Boult on Music

TOCCATA
PRESS

BOULT

ON

MUSIC

Words from a Lifetime's Communication

Foreword by
BERNARD SHORE

Introduction by
VERNON HANDLEY

Musicians on Music No. 1
Published by
TOCCATA PRESS
1983

This collection first published in 1983
by Toccata Press
© Lady Boult, the British Broadcasting Corporation,
Vernon Handley and Bernard Shore.

British Library Cataloguing in Publication Data
Boult, *Sir* Adrian
  Boult on music.—(Musicians on music, ISSN 0264-6889; no.
  1)
  1. Music
  I. Title   II. Series
  780′.92′4   ML160

ISBN 0 907689 03 5 (cased edition)
ISBN 0 907689 04 3 (paperback edition)
ISSN 0264–6889

Set in 11 on 12 point Baskerville by
Alan Sutton Publishing Ltd, Gloucester.
Printed and bound by
The Thetford Press Ltd, Thetford, Norfolk.

Contents

Two: ON CONDUCTORS

Five: ON MUSIC IN GENERAL

THE ART OF SIR ADRIAN

A Tribute from

BERNARD SHORE, C.B.E.

I had the immense privilege of a long personal friendship and years of working with Sir Adrian Boult, from those days as a student at the Royal College of Music, in his conducting class, right through those wonderful years of the 1930's, and rejoice to see him at last recognised as one of this century's really great conductors. It seems amazing that until he reached the age of about seventy he was not fully recognised, although most of us in the B.B.C. Symphony Orchestra had no doubt whatever that he had those rare gifts which would inevitably bring him to the top. It is one of the most refreshing thoughts that one who is an idealist, who hates all limelight and showmanship, can nevertheless achieve the highest fame; and his last years in the recording studio proved that advanced age can bring increasing rather than declining powers — a splendid and sparkling crown to a dedicated life.

One tends to divide famous conductors into two groups. The first are the virtuosi, who concentrate on the finest and most brilliant orchestral playing, using the composer, seemingly, as a vehicle for their own virtuosity. The second group are the idealists, whose whole aim is to get as near as possible to the composer's mind. It is they who seem to shed a new light on a great work, however well-known it may be. It is to this group, of course, that Boult belonged; and it is in this group that are found the conductors whom we call really great. Sir Adrian spent all his life in the deep study of every score he conducted, searching for the innermost thoughts of the composer, past or present, and listening to the interpretations of all the great conductors from Nikisch to Toscanini. In the orchestra we were always conscious of his utter concentration on the music and his self-effacement — all part of his manner on the rostrum, which is the exact opposite to those conductors who nearly throw themselves at the orchestra, intent on impressing their own vivid personality and brilliance on the audience. His quiet stance on the platform, the rigid economy of his gestures and general stillness were grossly misunderstood in the 1930's by those who thought that only the wildest movements on the rostrum could wake the orchestra to its full power. I even heard it said that Boult was dull!

The art of Sir Adrian was at its most impressive in works with a great sense of architecture because his mind seemed to brood over a score from a height, surveying all the essential features, like the peaks of a mountain range seen from afar. But he never lost sight of the highest peak of all. There was always a focal point towards which he would drive remorselessly; and if the orchestra let go too soon, or sagged when he got there, the players would soon hear about it. There is a terrific moment in the first movement of Elgar's Second Symphony, where at the height of climax the composer puts a slash across the score, for a moment of breathtaking silence. At such a moment Boult was in his element. He built up tension to its breaking point, and then, with stark clarity, came the flash, as of vivid lightning, and the orchestra exploded into the grand Elgarian flood of sound. All was achieved with just an incisive flick of the stick and one of his rare left-arm gestures — unmistakable to every eye. Incidentally, Elgar himself always fluffed that difficult moment, although we adored playing with him — it seemed just beyond his power of conducting.

One of Boult's particular attitudes towards the orchestra, like Montgomery's to his soldiers of the Eighth Army, was that he took the players into his confidence, treating them as fine artists in their own right. He expected them all to use their intelligence and not to have to tell them what to listen to. One typical comment at rehearsal occurred in the slow movement of Brahms' Fourth Symphony when the players were slack. An angry remark stopped everything at once. 'How on earth can you expect the clarinet to play his tune decently when you are lumbering along underneath like that?

For goodness' sake, *listen* and keep alive!' Mild enough words, but not very mild in voice.

Orchestral balance was almost an obsession with him, and we often wished, in the old days of broadcasting, that he wouldn't so often consult the balance and control department of the B.B.C. — but he was right, because he was always conscious that if the concert was broadcast then he must be certain that the balance was not only right for the hall but also for the microphone.

One question of balance for which Sir Adrian is renowned is that he always had the second violins facing the firsts, instead of the more usual plan of having the violins together in one block. When foreign conductors came to conduct we often had to play a game of musical chairs before settling down to rehearse. I remember when Koussevitzky got up on the rostrum the first time he arrived, he looked round the orchestra, glared at the second violins, remarked 'Eet eez imposseeble!' — and just walked off! But Boult had extremely good reasons for his plan. First of all, it gives the second violins their own character — as violins sound slightly different in colour when turned away from the audience, as long as players sit up properly. There are many instances of firsts and seconds answering each other, where their slightly different colour enhances the music: for instance, the second violins in the opening of the storm in the *Pastoral* Symphony of Beethoven sound exactly right — a little frightened without the support of the firsts on the other side of the orchestra, and with the orchestral leader glaring at them like a headmaster! And secondly, of course, the sound of the violins is spread right across the orchestra instead of all on one side. In his book *Thoughts on Conducting,*[1] Sir Adrian wrote:

> In almost every symphony from Mozart to Elgar can be found passages where the two groups answer each other, phrase by phrase; these are completely ineffective when the reply is just a pale reflection coming from the depths of the firsts instead of asserting itself from the front of the platform.

But there were very few matters like this on which he insisted. In general he seemed able to adjust himself to any

1. Phoenix Books, London, 1963.

situation, without the slightest difficulty, where others would
refuse, or be unable to cope. Most conductors require space to
move about on, but Boult just required room on which to put
his feet, which never seemed to move at all. (At the coronation
of King George VI, up on the Rood Screen of Westminster
Abbey, he had exactly room to place his feet, with a 40-foot
drop behind him; yet he appeared completely free and
untroubled.)

One characteristic of a Boult rehearsal was his insistence
on 'rhythmic swing'. Scarcely a rehearsal took place without
resort to this expression. Nothing so much exasperated him as
a wooden accent bumping on the first note of each bar. Take,
for instance, a work like Beethoven's *Leonora* Overture No. 3,
after the introduction when first violins and 'cellos start off the
Allegro. After the first few bars he would complain: 'No, no, it
all sounds dead. Do swing the rhythm over the bar lines —
from the end of the second to the third bar and so on — and *do*
mind that great crescendo — those last four bars are only *forte*
and *then* comes the almighty crash at the end!' Another
example of this 'rhythmic swing' can be heard in his recording
of Bach's Third Brandenburg Concerto. The terrific momen-
tum he obtained gave the first and last movements not only
immense vitality, but one could almost feel the grand swing of
some gigantic pendulum.

It was characteristic of Sir Adrian's art that he could not
stand slackness in any vital rhythmic feature. There is a
dangerous example of this, particularly for the strings, in the
first movement of Beethoven's Seventh Symphony, after flute
and oboe have shown them 'how to play it'. This rhythmic
figure always comes off clearly in the wind, but for instance,
when the strings take over later on, he was for ever chiding us,
and complaining that the last quaver came too soon, and the
whole essence of the tight rhythm was lost.

Another priority was style. The cultivation of the sense of
style characteristic of the composer formed a very important
part of his training of the orchestra. The difference in playing
might be subtle, but he insisted that the great breadth of a
Brahms phrase must be quite different from that which is
required for a French composer, where meticulous neatness
and compactness of phrase are necessary. His recordings

afford two examples: compare the great tune in the Finale of the C minor Symphony of Brahms, where you can feel its immense breadth and space, with a tune similar in a way, the principal theme from the finale of César Franck's Symphony in D minor, and you will observe how he keeps strictly to time and meticulous phrasing to conform with the French style. On the other hand, with the Russian School everything would be more exaggerated, with violent changes of mood and colour.

Sir Adrian always had the utmost consideration for the players, fully understanding their irritation at vain repetition in rehearsal. If he wanted a passage repeated he would explain precisely why. His general method of rehearsing, for a symphony for instance, was to play as far as the end of the exposition without stopping. Then he would comment on certain salient points — and if one department was at fault, then he took them alone, with the rest of the orchestra at rest. Rehearsals were just a means to an end: he might require full power, at times, for the purpose of balance, but it was the performance that mattered. It was very noticeable that he let himself go only on the night, and then demanded everything we had — but not before. What a contrast to all those conductors who drive like mad at rehearsals and have nothing extra to give at performance! He would be apt to say at a final rehearsal: 'First horn, I don't want you to spoil your lip now, but mind — everything you've got tonight!'

Boult's stick could only be matched by the late Sir Henry Wood. He used it as an extra limb of his own body, and the point of his stick was the focal point of every player's eye. It is curious that of all the conductors I have ever played with (or seen for that matter), only Henry Wood and Adrian Boult ever seem to have made an exhaustive study of the technique and control of the stick. Surely if a conductor is going to use a stick, why shouldn't he learn to use it, as we have to master our instruments in the orchestra? All fine instrumentalists never make an unnecessary movement, which is precisely why Boult never made an unnecessary movement; his stick did it for him. It was held as lightly in the fingers as a string player's bow, and was always in complete control. It moved to and from a focal point always visible to the whole orchestra, and gave him an extra and extremely sensitive instrument to work

with. In *pianissimo* passages nothing moved but the point of
the stick, controlled by two fingers and a thumb. (It is true
that this movement was occasionally so small that players on
the fringe of the orchestra sometimes suffered extreme anxiety
in trying to spot the movement, but it worked!) This, of
course, gave him an enormous range from the quietest to the
most colossal sound. When he was building up power, he
gradually brought his right arm — a very long one — into
action and at the height of climax his left hand would punch
home like the fist of a heavy-weight boxer. The point is that
his left hand was always completely free for expression or
emphasising points and for any particular department he was
concerned with. It was completely independent from the stick,
which was the orchestra's dynamo. The orchestra suffers so
many conductors who pump both arms up and down
together, the stick being merely a spike fastened to their right
hand.

Boult's stillness on the rostrum was very deceptive. All
famous conductors from either of our two groups, virtuosi or
idealists, hold the orchestra with their eyes; and behind
Boult's stick technique came that vital strength and power
from his own eyes, but with him there was nothing to distract
the players from their job — they just played, and were left to
play, to the utmost of their ability, but at any moment ready
for any spontaneous demand.

I well remember his remarks to the orchestra (made at a
rehearsal of Schubert's Great C major Symphony, one of his
very finest interpretations, in the closing stages of the finale)
when dealing with the building-up of a climax, and have never
ceased to pass them on to all students: 'Orchestra, that
crescendo never really grew at all. You had used everything
up before you got to the *fortissimo*, which incidentally was a
very poor affair, and I want still more power five bars later.
Don't crescendo immediately you see it marked — play softer
if you like. Remember how far you have to go, and make an
absolutely steady pile up to the crash at the *fortissimo* — and at
the *sempre fortissimo* five bars later, all you're worth!'

Boult had a thing about the accompaniment of orchestral
soloists, who are always endeared to a conductor who looks
after them. He would explain what he wanted as regards

colour, phrasing, and so on, at rehearsal; yet at the performance he would never 'conduct' a soloist, but look to the
accompaniment, so that the soloist would be free to express
himself. This attitude would produce wonderful results. We
used to be proud of our soloists in the B.B.C. Symphony
Orchestra, as their artistry was superb, and they would rise to
considerable heights.

As for accompanying soloists in general, Boult set a new
tradition in this country for accompanying piano concertos.
Until the 1930's the conductor generally stood between
audience and piano, but this upset his idea of balance, as the
power of the open piano in front of him was far too prominent
in his ears for finding the right orchestral balance. So he
invariably conducted behind the piano, and then not only
heard a more finely balanced sound, but, typical of Sir
Adrian, he was able to efface himself, so that there was
nothing between soloists and audience to distract. When
accompanying it was fascinating to watch the point of that
stick, following the soloist round as if magnetised. He seemed
to be guiding the orchestra into the soloist's hands. He would
never, even with inexperienced young students, impose his
will on them, but would accompany, as he would a great
artist.

I can never remember any conductor who could give a
finer production of a new and difficult work. First Boult would
do everything he could to study it with the composer, to
ensure the right mood, tempi, orchestral colour, and so on. To
take an extreme case, for the first performance of a concert
version of Berg's *Wozzeck*, he invited Kurt Preraurer from
Berlin, who had produced the opera there, to attend all
rehearsals, so that everything possible was done to get every
note as the composer wished.

Another unforgettable instance was the first performance
of Vaughan Williams' Fourth Symphony. This fearsome work
staggered all musicians, and particularly those who knew
their beloved Vaughan Williams best. Instead of what we
might have expected after the *Pastoral* Symphony, this frightful tornado suddenly burst over the orchestra — the very devil
seemed to be let loose. It is extremely difficult for both
orchestra and conductor; but I can still see Boult on the

rostrum, completely cool, clear, level-headed, with Vaughan
Williams stalking up to the platform looking somewhat bewildered himself. And, of course, the actual performance of this
new and great work was superb.

Stravinsky's *Rite of Spring* was considered a tough nut to
crack in the 1930's, and several foreign conductors made a
terrible fuss of its difficulties and the orchestra's shortcomings;
yet Boult directed us in this work in Paris, that veritable
sanctum of Stravinsky, without the slightest sense of strain or
fuss of any kind.

One of Boult's very early productions was Holst's *The
Planets*, always a great fillip to an orchestra's skills. He
conducted the first performance in 1918, and made musical
history. Even this early in his career, our finest musicians —
like Sir Hubert Parry, Sir Henry Wood, Vaughan Williams —
recognised his outstanding gifts and personal integrity. Holst
was quite determined that it should be Boult who first
performed *The Planets*.

When Boult first took command of the B.B.C. Symphony
Orchestra and became Director of Music of the B.B.C. in
1930, he led us into a new era. It was the first time London
had had a permanent salaried orchestra, hand-picked from
throughout the United Kingdom under its own conductor. Of
course, its duties included playing at the Promenade Concerts
under Sir Henry Wood, and here again the standard immediately rose, because the concerts were more adequately
rehearsed. The introduction of the Wednesday Symphony
Concerts set an entirely new standard of orchestral playing.
Typical of Boult, utterly unselfish, he was determined that his
orchestra should have the most wonderful experience of
working with the finest conductors of the world; and that
decade from 1930 to the outbreak of the war brought a new art
to orchestral playing. It was because of Sir Adrian's general
training in style, and his bringing all the players to a fuller
understanding of the music, that the orchestra seldom experienced trouble from any of the famous conductors who came to
work with us, including the great Toscanini himself. When
Toscanini, then the supreme living conductor, came for the
first time to conduct the B.B.C. Symphony Orchestra in 1935,
he left practically untouched two works, Elgar's *Enigma*

Variations and Brahms's Fourth Symphony. What a tribute to Boult's training! Yet in those days only a few recognised his genius, while in his last years Sir Adrian was almost by himself in the world.

It may indeed be said that Sir Adrian Boult led this new era as no one else could have done; and all who took part owe him an enormous debt, as the memories of those great ten years will never fade. As I wrote at the beginning of this essay, Boult was unsurpassed in the art of true interpretation. His whole life was dedicated to the aim of getting the music over to the audience in a shape as near as possible to the composer's mind, through deep and continual study of scores, scholarship, and mastery of his own technique, which must never distract the audience but be crystal clear to the orchestra. Few conductors, if any, could surpass him in the whole vast range of the classics, on which he frequently shed new light; while his prodigious contribution to modern music speaks for itself — 146 first performances of new works between 1931 and 1971 alone.

Boult's art of interpretation is now safe for posterity thanks to the vast number of recordings he made. Indeed, it seems amazing that such an idealist should win the Golden Disc, awarded by E.M.I. for the sale of a million discs and which had previously been won only by the Beatles! And these records were only part of the story, since other recording companies were concerned as well. (We are indebted to Alan Sanders for the complete discography.[2]) Amongst his beloved classics there are the six Brandenburg Concertos of Bach, five of the Beethoven Symphonies, all of the Brahms and Schumann Symphonies, Nos. 3 and 4 of Mendelssohn, and, of course, the Schubert Great C major, one of the greatest interpretations of all time. But alas, there is no recording of the Bach B minor Mass nor the *St. Matthew Passion* which we remember as so outstanding.

There is a long list of British composers who have reason to be grateful for the intense care he took of their works and the number of them that he committed to record, including all the

2. *Sir Adrian Boult: A Discography*, General Gramophone Publications, Harrow, 1981.

major orchestral and choral works of Elgar, Vaughan Williams, Holst, Ireland, and a good number of those of Bax, Walton, Bliss, Howells, Butterworth, and many others; and not long before his retirement, he revived several of Parry's finest works.

Boult was a conductor who needed and loved his own orchestra and never sought international stardom, with its travelling all over the world. When he was 'retired' from the B.B.C. (not its finest hour!), instead of thinking of some glamorous and lucrative appointment overseas, he gave his magnificent services to the London Philharmonic Orchestra when it was facing difficult times.

He was a gifted administrator, and in those critical years from 1930 to 1940 he fought and won the battle for music in the B.B.C., on top of all his work with the Symphony Orchestra.

No, we shall not see his like again, for many reasons. First, there was his great personal integrity, which never allowed him to break his word. If he promised to conduct an amateur orchestral or choral society, no engagement he was offered, however important, would ever tempt him away. In all things, his word was truly his bond. Then there was his hatred of showmanship and love of self-effacement, so as to avoid any interference between audience and music. Next came his deep consideration for the orchestra and the players' skills and artistry. He was always careful at rehearsal never to drive too hard, but to leave plenty of reserve for the concert. Finally there was his stillness on the rostrum and complete control of every movement, from a simple flick of the wrist in *pianissimo* to an enormous heave of both arms to their impressive length at the height of a climax, with the point of the stick invariably the focal point for all eyes.

The combination of these characteristics of Boult is very rare, except in the very greatest of his colleagues, but they were all deeply embedded in that tall, upright figure, with eyes that would command and a rich, warm voice which inspired, but never irked, at rehearsal. In his manners, speech

3.   The whole of this fascinating story is well told in the excellent *B.B.C. Symphony Orchestra* by Nicholas Kenyon, B.B.C. Publications, London, 1980.

and bearing Sir Adrian Boult seems to represent the finest
type of English gentleman, fully aware of current events but
reminding us of the best of our great heritage of nation and
music. His name will surely always remain among the greatest
of our musicians.

Bernard Shore

INTRODUCTION
VERNON HANDLEY

Private man though Sir Adrian Boult was, it was inevitable that someone who lived as long in the public eye as he did and who held the offices that came his way, should have been required to speak and write. With the exception of his small *Handbook on the Technique of Conducting*[1] one feels that he used words almost reluctantly; this would be entirely in keeping with his approach to conducting, which contained a rare element of self-effacement, and his belief that once a conductor had conducted he had had his say. Most of what he wrote and said in broadcasts was dismissed as 'too mild', and this Introduction seeks only to prevent the reader of *Boult on Music* from presuming that here are the bland statements of a man intent on avoiding controversy.

The editor has been meticulous in his choice, placing the pieces included here so that subjects encompass extracts designed both for broadcasts and for books, rather than dividing the collection into broadcasts, talks and writings; and, inevitably, there is some degree of repetition, although editing has removed what it can. Most of these pieces were, of course, written to be heard on the air rather than seen on the page and yet, although miscellanies of this sort are bound to seem 'bitty', at least in part, Boult's writing and his broadcasting technique were very close, for his written style, if not colourful, often contained the small colloquialisms that made his broadcasting less formal. If the reader never heard Sir Adrian speak, it would not be a bad idea to imagine a light, clear voice, serious, but carefully modulated so as to allow an occasional chuckle (speaking *is* the basis of this book). Westminster and Oxford had not produced an exaggerated accent, and only an occasional dated slang expression betrayed the

---

1.   First published for private circulation at the Royal College of Music in 1920; 2nd impression, Hall, Oxford, 1937; revised edn., Paterson, London, 1968.

great man's educational background and his age, for listening
to a broadcast made when he was in his seventies would have
led the listener to believe that a forty-year-old was speaking.

It is his ability to assess all subjects and to distill from
them the essential characteristics that presents the greatest
problem in dealing with Boult the writer or broadcaster. For
instance, his analysis of Schubert's C major Symphony, given
as an interval talk on the Home Service in December 1943, is
an exercise any musicologist could have done; indeed, any
musician would have chosen the examples Sir Adrian did. But
how many, having finished their description of the last
movement with metaphors (unusual for Boult) describing the
emotional force of his last example, would then prosaically
point out that it is the *structural* basis of classical movements
that makes them work, rather than the tunes themselves.

The danger in reading Boult is the danger we all faced in
watching him conduct. It all seems so naturally undramatic
and flowing that we cannot believe important points are being
made; and unfortunately in reading these pieces we do not
have the impact of the music he made to secure our concentration. A composer friend of mine once said that Sir Adrian's
short remarks, seemingly thrown away, would constantly
come back to him, sometimes months later, containing the key
to some very important part of his thinking or development.
The reader would be well advised to have all his faculties
about him when reading Boult's account whether of Ravel or
of Nikisch's rehearsal methods. The effort one must make to
read between the lines whenever Sir Adrian is talking about
himself is considerable, for there were certain doors through
which he wished no-one to pass. This was an attitude which
helped him in simplification, which he held to be an important
attitude for him, both as conductor and as man. Sir Adrian's
Handbook on the Technique of Conducting begins with the words:
'The object of technique in all art is the achievement of the
desired end with the greatest simplicity and economy of
means'. So perhaps simplification is the wrong word, for
almost all these pieces try to concentrate on the fundamental
aspects of the subject, whatever it was: the reader should not
search for new ideas from this great man; rather, he should
find in Sir Adrian's example a reminder to think a subject

through in order to discover its basic truths. In this he did all of us who follow music an immense service.

I remember once, after I had been to a whole series of his rehearsals, that we were talking together in a London park. Our conversation, which lasted half-an-hour and during which he consumed four ice-creams, ended with his telling me that it was high time that I went to the rehearsals of a certain other conductor. I answered curtly that I had already been to this particular maestro. Sir Adrian gave me a side-long glance and said, 'Ah well, you don't need to go again, do you?' It told me all I needed to know about his assessment of the conductor involved and his recognition of the stage of thinking at which I had arrived.

Sir Adrian rarely made any remark on conducting or the arts in general that did not proceed from deep and long consideration of those subjects. He conducted 'on principle', as he said, rather than on whim, and principles guided him when writing or broadcasting. But, as we all know, principles often conflict sharply with acceptable behaviour and Boult the principled artist was occasionally at odds with Boult the perfect gentleman. He was able more successfully than most of us to resolve this conflict in his public utterances, and the turmoil this must have caused in him was rarely revealed. In only two areas were signs of that conflict shown. Just occasionally, and privately, he would express himself in uncompromising terms about matters of principle, but publicly it was only in rare flashes of temper, usually immensely enjoyed by the members of orchestras, that anything but the perfect gentleman was glimpsed.

In a miscellany of this sort Sir Adrian cannot be caught off-guard. Most of the pieces included were written for later broadcast and so the gentleman has the upper hand; thus an inspection of any person, composer, conductor is attempted with the utmost tact and generosity. There is a marked difference when the subject is abstract. The care in the latter case is for a simplicity of expression which may lead the reader to think that nothing profound has been stated. When one reads material designed to be heard rather than read and which covers five decades of a great man's life, one must be careful to read each piece with one's mind like Lamb's clerk in the South Sea House, 'in its original state of white paper'. An example of the kind of contrast one must appreciate would be to compare Boult's warm and generous tribute to Beecham — with whose interpretations he was often entirely out of sympathy — with his justification of his own orchestral seating plan, where the clearest exposition of the subject is delivered and no-one spared. In both cases, however, simple expression is at the service of a genuine politeness, or a great clarity of vision.

Vernon Handley

24

ACKNOWLEDGEMENTS

We are much indebted to the following people who have
helped in the production of *Boult on Music*: for the provision of
much of the source material Mrs. Jacqueline Kavanagh and
her staff at the B.B.C.'s Written Archives Centre, Caversham;
for advice on copyright Anne Vie, Permissions and Rights,
B.B.C. Publications; the B.B.C. for waiving any publication
fee for the pre-1950 material that remains B.B.C. copyright;
for assistance and encouragement Mrs. Gwen Beckett, for
many years Sir Adrian's secretary, and Lady Boult; Anthony
F. Leighton Thomas, Editor of *The Music Review*, for permission to reprint the Nikisch article from its pages; *Music and
Letters* for permission to use a further Nikisch article; the
Schools Music Association for the article on Havergal Brian;
Michael Pope who, when at the B.B.C., produced the programme by Bernard Shore (strangely, it was never broadcast)
which formed the basis of his Foreword; Robert Layton for
permission to use part of his interview with Sir Adrian on
Vaughan Williams; Duncan Johnson, Librarian of the Royal
College of Organists, for providing a copy of Sir Adrian's
lecture on Elgar's Symphony No. 2; for advice and suggestions
Robert Simpson (whose First Symphony was given its U.K.
première and recorded by Sir Adrian), Miron Grindea,
Michael Kennedy, Alan Watkins, Robert Matthew-Walker of
Phoenix Records, David Brown of the Havergal Brian Society,
and Christopher Morris of Oxford University Press; for
bibliographical assistance, the staffs of the Central Music
Library, O.U.P., Novello and the British Institute of Recorded Sound; and for help with proof-reading Sue Rose and
David Brown. And the support and encouragement of Bernard Shore and Vernon Handley went far beyond the warmth
and willingness with which they provided their contributions.
The debt we owe Sir Adrian is, of course, enormous, and this
collection was intended to go a very small way towards
repaying it. Typically modestly, he said that he found the
suggestion of this book 'a great honour'. It should have been
paid him earlier.

MARTIN J. ANDERSON
TOCCATA PRESS

PART ONE
ON COMPOSERS

<hr>

BACH
Mass in B Minor

This talk was originally given in March 1938, as part of one of Sir Adrian's regular talks on 'Music of the Week'. Early music enthusiasts may reflect that although far more is known of the minutiae of early music interpretation than over forty years ago when Sir Adrian gave this talk, he shows a sensitivity to the spirit of Bach's work, a desire to get as close to the original as possible that are wholly in accord with modern attitudes to interpretation.

This week we have on our programme that great masterpiece, Bach's B minor Mass. I often feel that our broadcasting programmes ought to include every year the B minor Mass, the *St. Matthew* and *St. John Passions*, *Israel in Egypt*, the *Messiah*, Beethoven's great *Missa Solemnis*, and perhaps *The Creation* and other works of Haydn and Brahms' *German Requiem*. Perhaps some day we may be able to achieve this for you, though at present we are prevented by difficulties both in the matter of balance as between this and that form of music broadcasting, and in the matter of securing adequate performances of such great works.

It is interesting to reflect that something like sixty years ago the B minor Mass had never been heard in this country and it was necessary to form a society specially for the study and performance of it. Jenny Lind and her husband, Otto Goldschmidt, founded the Bach Choir for this purpose, and the honourable tradition of the choir certainly is splendidly

maintained in their performances of this work, but in other
things too, notably their annual performance of the *St.
Matthew Passion* on Passion Sunday.

The music of Johann Sebastian Bach presents a good
many special problems to the interpreter. To begin with, in
Bach's scores there are very few dynamics, and so most of the
expression must be determined by the performer from internal
evidence. New editions are published from time to time giving
editors' interpretations, but most editors who have set their
hands to Bach would, I think, be ready to admit that any
interpreter has a right to change their suggestions if he feels
minded to do so. But the mere question of volume is not by
any means the whole of the problem. Perhaps the greatest of
all is that known to musicians as the realisation of the
continuo. Let me explain this term. In Bach's time the
number of performers was very much smaller than it is now.
There was no conductor, and Bach himself if he was taking
charge of a performance would sit at the organ or the
harpsichord and direct affairs from there. It was not the
custom to write out an organ or harpsichord part complete
except when it partook of the nature of a solo — usually the
keyboard part is a single line in the bass clef, which is called
the continuo part. There are figures written over the notes to
indicate the kind of chord which is to be played above it,
roughly speaking, by the right hand of the performer, and it is
up to the keyboard performer to decide how to space out
those chords and whether to break them into arpeggios, and
so on.

Now the knowledge that this keyboard performer was
going to fill out the chords in this way made it unnecessary for
Bach to see that every chord was otherwise complete in his
score, and it is often to be observed that if you play a Bach
score as it stands without filling out the bass part as indicated
by these figures, you will notice a certain number of empty
gaps. These gaps would normally be filled by the keyboard
player if he realised his figures in the proper way, and as
nowadays the art of playing the figured bass is not practised
much, it is usual to prepare a part for the organ or the
harpsichord, which is played by someone other than the
conductor. The conductor now having to manage a much

larger number of people, he uses a stick instead of being able just to direct them from his own playing on the keyboard instrument.

Again, it is up to the conductor or editor to decide when to use an organ for the continuo and when to use a harpsichord. In our performance on Wednesday I have tried to make that decision according to the character of the music, and I hope you will feel that it is appropriate in each case. The contrast in the character of solos and choruses is most marked in the B minor Mass. It is rare for any soloist to be accompanied by more than a small handful of instruments and, of course, the continuo, while the full orchestra is generally used to accompany the chorus.

But Bach's full orchestra is not the full orchestra of Beethoven and the more modern composers. There are no trumpets [*sic!*] and there are no clarinets. Bach's oboes and bassoons were much more powerful instruments than those of today. This has caused some editors to add clarinets more or less in unison with the oboes, but the resulting tone is unpleasant, and we hope by using rather more players than usual to put the oboe line before you in its original quality.

Another interesting point in regard to the B minor Mass is that in the great complete edition of the works of Bach which began publication some eighty years ago they did not have the autograph manuscript of the Mass at their disposal, as this was the property of a private owner who refused to lend it. They accordingly published the B minor Mass as a result of a collation of several later scores and some of the separate instrumental parts which were used in Bach's time, and unfortunately a number of inaccuracies crept in. The original manuscript subsequently found its way into the Berlin National Library where it now is. About five years ago a facsimile of that great score was published and has been of enormous value to those of us who are keen to get as pure a text as possible as a basis for our work. A good many of the modifications simply affect a note or two here and there, but a few of them are more important than this. For instance, Sir Donald Tovey, in examining the lovely duet for soprano and tenor, 'Domine Deus', No. 7, discovered that the flute part which was marked as for a solo flute in the original printed part is in the manuscript clearly shown in the plural for flutes in unison.[1]

The beauty of this obbligato played by five or six flutes in unison is quite extraordinary. Sir Donald has also noticed[2] that the solo instrument that plays in the tenor solo towards the end of the work, 'Benedictus qui venit', which had always been assumed to be a solo violin, is not marked as such in the manuscript. He holds the theory that a flute solo was here meant. We have tried it with a flute, but I must confess I rather prefer the warm tone of the solo violin, and that is what we shall use next Wednesday.

I think these examples will show that a great deal more is involved in the performance of a work by Bach than in the straight playing of a work, say, by Elgar, where the composer's intentions are clearly shown on paper and the interpreter's task is, first, to see that these are faithfully carried out, and, second, to bring the work to life.

BRIAN

Gothic Symphony

In the Royal Albert Hall, on 30 October 1966, Sir Adrian conducted the first professional performance of Havergal Brian's massive *Gothic* Symphony, in the presence of the 90-year-old composer. This article is reproduced from *Music* (Vol. 1, No. 2, Spring 1967), the journal of the Schools Music Association.

The name of Havergal Brian has been known to me pretty well all my life, as I am thirteen years younger than he is, and in the early years of the century there were not so many

1. *Essays in Musical Analysis*, Vol. 5, *Vocal Music*, Oxford University Press, London, 1937, p. 32; reprinted in *Concertos and Choral Works*, O.U.P., London, 1981.
2. *ibid.*, p. 49.

composers about, so that those who were there were pretty conspicuous. His name was to be seen in catalogues, and occasionally on concert programmes, though I cannot remember actually hearing any of his work myself.

Sir Granville Bantock, who was very kind to me when I first went to Birmingham in my middle thirties, spoke very enthusiastically of Mr. Brian's work, and asked me to think about the inclusion of something in our programmes. Our Birmingham repertoire was very much limited in those days. Devoted chiefly to the 'main stream of music' we had little space for anything else; in fact, I can remember only very occasional appearances of Bantock himself, Vaughan Williams, Bax, Holst, Mahler and Bartók, outside the main repertoire.

It is a surprise to me, looking back on my years with the B.B.C., that Brian's name did not come up for consideration;[1] the most all-embracing machinery was devised for examining music, new and old, and bringing forward things that we felt were entirely neglected, but it only shows how there can be unexpected gaps in the most careful planning, and it is a great calamity that our staff then did not include a man like Dr. Robert Simpson, whose influence on the B.B.C. has been felt in his championship of Nielsen in particular, while he remains silent about the splendid music which he himself composes.

After a performance in February 1954 of Brian's Eighth Symphony, which I conducted, it was only in 1966 that Dr. Simpson succeeded in securing performances of the *Sinfonia Tragica*, Symphony No. 10, and four or five of the others, and of the great *Gothic* (No. 2[2]) in October. I was honoured to be invited to conduct it, particularly as Dr. Simpson promised to look after what might be called the secretarial side of the conductor's job. A good deal has been said of the enormous size of the orchestra and choir employed. This is believed to be

1. In fact, there were a few B.B.C. performances of orchestral works by Brian in the 1930's, and in 1944 Sir Adrian himself conducted two of the Symphonic Dances from Brian's burlesque opera, *The Tigers*.
2. In 1967 Brian renumbered his earlier Symphonies, admitting the *Sinfonia Tragica* (now No. 6) to the numbered canon; *The Gothic* then became No. 1, displacing *A Fantastic Symphony* of which the two central movements are missing.

due to the suggestion of Sir Henry Wood that Havergal Brian should write a work which would exploit the sonorities of the different groups in the orchestra, so that with eleven clarinets of different kinds, to take an example, every kind of timbre could be heard.

The examination of the parts (which inevitably contained many misprints), the preparation of the choral scores (a labour of great complexity), and the marshalling of the choral forces were all taken over by Dr. Simpson. This involved a good deal of correspondence with four separate conductors outside the B.B.C. staff, and much office work, with the organisation of all rehearsals — with or without the two outside brass bands — with or without the girls' and boys' choirs — and so on. I have never before seen the Maida Vale Studio of the B.B.C. set out as it was for our rehearsals with every inch of floor space covered with players and singers, and no room for any audience, if anyone besides Dr. Simpson, armed with another copy of the monumental score, had wished to be present.

The work is laid out symphonically, with the first three movements of similar dimensions to those, say, of a Brahms Symphony. But the composer calls them together Part I (35 minutes). Part II is, however, greatly extended and lasts over an hour in performance, being perhaps the longest setting of the *Te Deum* in existence. It is itself in three sections, of which the second is a setting of the single verse concerned with the Day of Judgment, the first and the third carrying the rest of the hymn. There are long passages of unaccompanied choral writing of immense difficulty — sometimes in as many as twenty separate parts, and we were fortunate to have so many singers who could tackle these difficulties, the seventy professionals of the B.B.C. Chorus being a tower of strength.

It was a proud experience to have the wonderful job of co-ordinating this great mass, and thanks to the elaborate and efficient preparation beforehand, the task was surprisingly easy. I used a stick an inch or two longer than usual (and the usual is pretty long!), and it was remarkable how clearly the Albert Hall platform allows even the most distant people to see the beat.

There was a moving scene at the close. The whole

audience knew that the ninety-year-old composer (who is now working on his Twenty-seventh Symphony) had, all through his life, with rare exceptions, been deprived of the experience of hearing his work, and many were deeply excited not only by the circumstances, but by the power of the music, and when he came on to the platform, and the audience stood up to applaud him, it seemed a fitting close to it all. It was an evening that none of us will ever forget.

BUTTERWORTH

Sir Adrian contributed this reminiscence of George Butterworth as a Foreword to the re-issue in 1948 of *George Butterworth, 1885-1916*. Both editions were published for private circulation only.

Soon after the horrors of the 1914 War, in which so many promising young men were sacrificed, Sir Alexander Kaye Butterworth compiled a book to which friends had contributed their impressions of his son, George Butterworth, composer, folk-dancer and soldier. The book was circulated among friends, but we now welcome a reprint of every word of it, with some valuable up-to-date additions which will increase its interest and usefulness.

There are probably few people living now who remember that quiet but impressive figure who was in the centre of London music, and was already in 1914 writing fine songs and other things. I didn't know him well, but his Oxford time finished in 1908 (when mine began), and after that he would often come to stay with Dr. and Mrs. Allen. Allen was then Professor of Music and Organist of New College. He later, as Sir Hugh Allen, became Director of the Royal College of Music in London. One night I happened to be at Allen's and George turned up pretty late, so he said he would go and get some supper at a nearby pub. I was on the way home and went with him, and as a rather green freshman was deeply impressed with the wisdom and knowledge of the older man.

It was, of course, an important event in his life when Arthur Nikisch conducted the first performance of his *A Shropshire Lad* at the Leeds Festival in 1913. I happened to be amongst the few people scattered about the Town Hall at the final rehearsal, and was sitting next to George as Nikisch, having finished the run-through, asked for his criticisms. George shook his head and thanked him: the performance had been exactly as he wished. Then he said quickly to me, 'You know, at the first rehearsal in London last week there were half-a-dozen small points I told him about. I was surprised that he didn't try any of them at the time, but he has remembered everything I said. I think that's pretty good'. That was indeed praise from one who was as critical of everyone (including himself). The performance, of course, made a deep impression.

ELGAR

I. As I knew him

This 'Personal Portrait' of Elgar was broadcast on the B.B.C.'s Overseas Service in May 1951.

I was brought up in Lancashire, near Liverpool, and I suppose it was as violent a change as any youngster could have to be sent to school at Westminster from such an environment. One of my first duties when I came home for the holidays was to go and call on an old lady who lived close to us, whose grandchildren were great friends of ours, and we were constantly in and out of each other's houses. She was a lovable, but rather formidable person who, like many others of her time, modelled herself on Queen Victoria, and was similarly feared by the young. On one of my visits she suddenly said to me, 'Adrian, do you know that my nephew, Frank Schuster, lives quite close to your school and like you is very fond of music? I shall write to him and ask him to invite you to his house. He has many musical friends and knows Dr. Elgar, the new composer, quite well, I believe'.

Mr. Schuster soon after that invited me to tea and then to one of his parties. He usually had eight or ten friends to dinner and then another dozen or so to come in afterwards and enjoy the music, in an ideally furnished music-room, round which the house seemed to be planned. It was an exciting moment when the guests came in from dinner — among them a German conductor, a famous Austrian singer, a well-known art critic and connoisseur, and the great Elgar himself. I was at once introduced to Elgar as 'the young man who goes to more concerts than you or I do', and the two of us were given seats in a corner with the newly issued full score of Elgar's *The Apostles*. He commented on the engraving, I remember, and showed me how marvellously spaced it all was, up and down its forty lines of music.

A young singer was among the guests that night — it was always Schuster's practice to mix the very famous with one or two promising youngsters. When her music-case was fetched our host discovered in it a song of Elgar's called *After*. Elgar was thereupon hauled away from the score of *The Apostles* and introduced to the young lady. When he heard what she was going to sing, he said in that half-joking, half-petulant way of his, which was so often misunderstood, 'Oh well, then, you've spoilt my evening for me'. When the song was over he said to me, 'Aren't the *words* beautiful?' How to answer that remark was a bit of a conversational problem for a lad of fourteen.

This kind of behaviour was characteristic of Elgar. I think there is a tendency among some Englishmen, particularly those connected with the arts, to imply that they aren't in the least interested in their jobs. And Elgar had this to a marked degree. Certainly there was nothing in his appearance to suggest the conventional idea of a musician. In fact, if you were told he was a country squire or retired army colonel, you would believe it.

He was of medium height and robust build. He had a fine head — striking and impressive, it seemed to me — with a strong aquiline nose and flowing moustache. His voice, I remember, was pleasant and rather quiet. When he was telling a story or speaking of something which interested him particularly, it all came out in rather a rush — the words tumbled over one another.

Except for a short period in London, he spent all his life in the country. By birth he belonged to the West of England — to Worcestershire. I think that beautiful district with its hills and valleys, orchards and woodlands must have influenced the musician. It certainly influenced the man. He was decidedly a countryman — fond of horses and keenly interested in race-meetings; fond of going for country walks with his beloved dogs; fond of growing things in his garden.

And besides these country pursuits he had a number of other interests. He was a tremendous reader — there wasn't much he hadn't read and read thoroughly. And he was particularly interested in science. Chemical experiments had a great fascination for him and at one time he had a laboratory fitted up in the attic of his house, where he narrowly escaped blowing himself up on several occasions.

I almost always had the luck, when meeting the great man, to find him in a good humour, when he would tell most entertaining stories about adventures of travelling in Italy in the pre-Mussolini days when they were extraordinarily happy-go-lucky, and of course showing his great love of the West Country. He would not often talk about music, making some ludicrous remark like 'I am not really interested in music; what I enjoy is horse-racing'. It was not always horse-racing; it might be his chemistry, or other things. More likely it would be books. I remember a tea-party at which he and Ernest Newman were competing with each other on the many out-of-the-way books that they had read.

He could be a brilliant talker in congenial company; but he also had an iron curtain which could come down with a heavy bang to shut out something for which he was not in the mood. In fact, there was a dogged, obstinate streak in him, and something that I can only call grumpiness. Once, when he was staying with friends, his host told him that a young singer — already making a name for himself — was coming to the house and was longing to meet Elgar. 'Oh Lord,' said Elgar, 'does that mean we're going to have music? If so, I'm going for a long walk.' And he did. It just so happened that on that occasion he was not in the mood for music or young musicians. Yet at other times he would go to immense trouble to help and encourage young artists, or to advise us on the interpretation of his own work.

In my own case, for instance, he took me carefully through the entire score of *In the South*, which I was including in some concerts in the Queen's Hall in 1918. I can still see him sitting at the piano with the score in front of him, giving me his comments as he turned over the pages. Another time, looking at the high B for solo trumpet, he said, 'let him hang on to that for as long as he likes'. He marked the score accordingly, showing just how long the trumpet might play. And I have that score still, with Elgar's notes on it. The same thing happened a few years later when I gave the first post-war performance of the Second Symphony. This time he came to the performance as well as the rehearsal, and sat in the old Queen's Hall in the artists' room doorway, behind the curtain.

About this time, too, he let me bring to his house a young Royal College student who was about to play Elgar's Violin Concerto with me at a College concert. He played it right through to the composer, who gave him, in the friendliest way, a good deal of guidance. 'There, I think, you might put more *con amore* into it,' he told him. Or, 'Now there's a brilliant show passage for you. Let them have it.'

His understanding of the potentialities of the various instruments of the orchestra is evident to anyone familiar with his work. It was, I think, partially due to the fact that he himself had played the trombone, bassoon and violin, and therefore had practical knowledge of the three categories — brass, wood and strings. This reminds me, by the way, of an occasion when Elgar and I were sitting in the gallery at the Queen's Hall, watching the orchestra come in. Suddenly Elgar nudged me and said, 'Listen to that trumpet'. I listened to the trumpeter warming up his instrument with some very complicated flourishes. 'If I had written that for him,' said Elgar, 'he would have said it was unplayable.'

He had a great affection and admiration for the British orchestras, all of which he had conducted in performances of his own works. He dedicated his *Cockaigne* Overture to 'my many friends, the members of British orchestras', and I remember a more intimate gesture at the last rehearsal of three concerts in which the B.B.C. made its tribute to his 75th birthday. I was conducting the rehearsal, and he twice said, 'Don't let any of them go away, Adrian. I want to come and speak to them when you have finished.' He came onto the platform and gave a most moving and charming speech of thanks to them for their support and friendship all his life.

His attitude to his public, on the other hand, was not always so affectionate. For instance, he never forgave Birmingham for its lukewarm reception of *Gerontius*. When, years later, I wanted to play it with a reduced orchestra he at first agreed, but when he heard we were performing in Birmingham he refused. Birmingham, he said grumpily, was full of rich people and they must pay for the full orchestra or not hear the work at all.

Among the other qualities of Elgar as I knew him were a liking for ceremonial occasions and a sense of fun. He loved dressing up, loved court dress, and was very proud of being Master of the King's Musick.

His sense of fun bubbled up, often unexpectedly, at any moment. I expect you all know the *Enigma* Variations — the most beloved of his more serious compositions — and you know how each of these Variations bears the initials or a nickname of one of his friends, and how the whole work is 'dedicated to my friends pictured within'. *Pictured* within is (as always with Elgar) the right word, for the different subjects are treated in different ways. There are character studies: C.A.E., that lovely, simple, quiet wife; the hearty squire who always banged the door; the two lovely sisters who lived in a beautiful old house which inspired that Variation perhaps more than the ladies, except that a twice-repeated peal of light laughter just touches a characteristic of one of them. There are sometimes just incidents of the friendship: for instance, G.R.S., organist of Hereford Cathedral, was walking with Elgar along the banks of the Wye with his bulldog, Dan. A stick was thrown into the water. Dan slid down the steep bank after it, and looked back at his master with a great bark. 'There now,' said G.R.S., 'set that to music, if you can.' Of course Elgar could, and did. Listen to the Variation: he slides down the bank, he paddles upstream, and then he barks — you can hear it all.

Incidentally, Elgar's own self-portrait is in the last Variation. He saw himself here in swashbuckling, swaggering noises of somewhat blatant vulgarity. But interwoven with this are the most subtle and beautiful harmonies taken from the first Variation — depicting his wife, and paying her the graceful compliment of showing her as the better part of himself.

One cannot speak of the *Enigma* Variations without thinking of 'Nimrod', one of Elgar's most intimate friends, Alfred Jaeger (called 'Nimrod' simply because 'Jäger' is German for 'hunter'). It is said that they were talking one day when Jaeger said he felt that the moderns were all moving too fast; no one could write a simple slow movement with real feeling in it, as Beethoven used to. Elgar took up the challenge, and produced one of his loveliest musical thoughts.

II. Symphony No. 2 in E flat

This is the text of a lecture given at the Royal College of Organists on 3 May 1947.

By way of introduction, I feel I must warn you, and perhaps apologise, in that I have made no attempt to bring to your notice many notable writings which are directly or indirectly concerned with this work. I feel that this is the student's own business, for no one can be said to have studied Elgar's Second Symphony who has not also studied at least the relevant chapters of Mr. Basil Maine's splendid study of Elgar,[1] and also Sir Donald Tovey's analysis.[2] Anyhow, the student will be expected to have thought out his own answers to the problems of the Symphony, and not just to quote the views of others.

'Dedicated to the Memory of his late Majesty King Edward VII. This symphony, designed early in 1910 to be a

1. Basil Maine, *Elgar: His Life and Works*, Bell's Musical Publications, London, 1933.
2. *op. cit.*, Vol. 2, *Symphonies 2* , Oxford University Press, London, 1936, pp. 114–121; reprinted in *Symphonies and Other Orchestral Works*, O.U.P., London, 1981.

loyal tribute, bears its present dedication with the gracious
approval of His Majesty the King.' Most dedications have so
little to do with the music that follows that they are easily
forgotten; but somehow I feel that these words form as
important a clue to the nature and to the understanding of this
great Symphony as the quotation from Shelley which stands
opposite the first page: 'Rarely, rarely, comest thou, spirit of
delight'. To begin with, the work lasts twice as long as many
modern symphonies, it is orchestrated with an opulence and
splendour that are truly Edwardian and regal, and the whole
treatment and the outlook are far removed from this war-
ridden age.

     The motto from Shelley gives us one of Elgar's much-
loved enigmas. What is the musical mood to be conveyed by
this quotation: 'Rarely, rarely, comest thou, spirit of delight'?
The 'spirit of delight' by itself is easy, of course, but how is
music to express the infrequency of its coming? And if that
infrequency is the crux of the situation, how is it that one critic
can label an important figure in the first movement as the
Spirit of Delight theme? It re-appears only once, in the coda of
the last movement, but in the first movement, at any rate, no
one could say it was heard 'rarely'.

     All this is intriguing, of course, but I must confess that I
don't really mind frightfully about it. Elgar could have told us
far more about it if he had wished, and he evidently didn't
wish. Perhaps I am specially incurious about such things, but
I always feel that music means so much that cannot be
translated into words, so much that in itself tells a story that is
not of our language, that there is not much point in trying to
drag it down to earth, and 'elucidate' it in such terms that
even if they help some listeners, they probably hinder, and
even irritate others. I don't mean that there isn't a great deal
that can be said to help people to listen to music. Sir Donald
Tovey and many others have shown us how it can be done,
and the way is definitely not to try and translate the meaning
of the music.

     At the beginning we plunge straight into the brilliance of
a Spring morning. Here, if anywhere, is the spirit of delight.
Now I think I should comment here on the surprising fact that
when the recapitulation comes, the whole second half of the

first subject group disappears altogether. Elgar's command of
the symphonic form is considerable, but I sometimes wonder
whether he always achieves the final inevitable solution in his
handling of a great movement — whether he can always
round off a work (as Sir Donald Tovey says) 'with astronomic-
al punctuality'. Be that as it may, he has provided many
wonderfully satisfactory and convincing structures, and he
has nearly achieved the impossible in the First Symphony:
basing a great work on the double foundation of A flat major
and D minor, the two ultimate opposites in key, separated as
they are by the tritone.

   Soon after the first subject group Elgar appears, surprisingly, to be leading us into G major for our second group. But
the new subject swings back into E flat, our tonic, and only
later we settle down to a lovely tune on the cello (which, Mr.
Ernest Newman has pointed out, is often played far too loud)
in the key of G minor, moving on again to the theme which we
thought might have been the beginning of the second group,
which turned out to be the transition. Elgar happily brings it
in again here as part of the second group and it piles up to a
noble climax which finishes our exposition.

   The development starts quietly and soon introduces us to
a new tune, which seems to me to bear as much importance as
the so-called Spirit of Delight, particularly when we look on
the Symphony as a whole. It brings an ominous tale of
mystery; and we must remember it as it first steals into our
consciousness on the 'cellos almost overlaid by a mass of
interesting things, as if the composer didn't wish us to take too
much notice of it. The Spirit of Delight is linked with the end
of it, and it is fully repeated in another key almost at once, and
the music crouches ready for a mighty effort. A long crescendo
follows and as often in symphonic first movements the moment of return to the tonic and first subject brings us a
passage of supreme brilliance.

   I have said that the recapitulation is ruthlessly cut down,
but not so much as to prevent Elgar from making some
delightful excursions into unexpected keys as we go along —
for instance, the quiet 'cello tune which was in G minor, is
now in F minor; but E flat is never far away, and the coda,
beginning quietly like the development, startles us by a

powerful outburst in terms of the opening bars of the movement, ending with a magnificent chromatic swirl on the horns.

Forgive me for referring again to earthly matters with
regard to the slow movement. It was, I have heard, written
after King Edward's death (although Basil Maine[3] says this is
not the case) — it might well be a funeral march. It has been
compared to the *Eroica* — for in both is something far greater
than mere personal sorrow, and I remember Sir Landon
Ronald saying of this movement, 'Of course you know all
about what it means?' I replied in the negative, whereat he
abruptly changed the conversation. I am afraid I may not
have sounded inquisitive enough. Anyhow, something of far
greater interest to me was a saying of Elgar himself (told me at
first hand). Pointing to the beginning of the return, he said, 'I
have no idea who wrote that down. I didn't — at any rate, I
remember nothing about it.' That seems to me a perfect
description of the inspiration which sometimes comes to those
who know what it means to get 'stuck', and to hammer out a
passage perhaps a dozen times or more; who know, in short,
the agony that is seen in Beethoven's sketchbooks. That
passage also epitomises the whole movement which is in pure
binary form (by Hadow's classification[4]). C minor is the tonic,
and the second group centres round F major. In the recapitulation it centres round E flat, but the coda takes us to C
major and finally to C minor.

The third movement, a ⅜ Scherzo, is headed 'Rondo'. It is
a highly developed rondo, the central episode of which is not
only the kernel of the movement, but perhaps even the
emotional kernel of the whole Symphony. We remember how
much the development of the first movement was occupied
with a new subject on the 'cellos, richly overlaid with many
other figures all over the orchestra? Well, now it comes again,
after a few tentative beginnings, and is one of the most
terrifying things I know in the whole of music. The composer
told me to be quite ruthless about the percussion here, and it
is sad that electric reproduction sometimes demands an
anaemic moderation from that lusty department. He said it

3. *op. cit.*
4. W.H. Hadow, *Sonata Form*, Novello, London, 1896.

must beat on the brain as in delirium, and I wondered if it had
come from his early association with the doctors and staff of
the asylum at Worcester. The movement ends in a brilliant C
major, an admirably balanced contrast to the impressive
opening of the Finale which follows.

I suppose it is natural that, as the shape of the classical
symphony developed, composers like Beethoven and Brahms
should feel that the final act of the drama should assume a
greater importance and a greater complexity than formerly.
Elgar has not hesitated to follow this scheme, and although
there is no actual likeness, I can't help remembering his
fondness for the Brahms F major. He used to conduct that
work with great insight, and although the finales are utterly
different, they do both finish on a note of glorious tranquillity,
and both codas have reference to falling themes taken from
their first movements. I always feel that applause should be
forbidden after these two magical closes, and I find that for
this reason, amongst others, cathedral performances always
seem to enhance their beauty.

The Spirit of Delight itself is not more elusive than the
mood of this opening. The simple theme is just full of
meaning, and I can find no words to describe it — it is quite
beyond language. The second subject swings its way all round
the string section and then concentrates in a great unison. I
can remember Elgar pointing to the passage with some gentle
remark that couldn't conceal his affection for it. The development is very stormy, with some quite formidable string
passages, and its restless modulations come to a check with a
climax in the surprising key of B minor. Textual students will
be interested to know that the composer used to ask his first
trumpet to extend his high B in the second bar of 149 as long
as he liked at this bar. He wrote the letters 'TR' in the margin
of my score with a long line after them. A long diminuendo
follows, at the end of which we find ourselves unexpectedly
floating down the main stream with that eloquent opening
tune on 'cellos and bassoons. The recapitulation is regular,
but a bar-by-bar comparison with the exposition shows an
interesting addition of a bar or two here and there, culminat-
ing at the final climax in a whole pile-up of new sequences
which intensely broaden the grandeur of this magnificent

movement. At the summit of the whole range, the eighth bar after 165, Elgar would add a 32- or 64-foot organ pedal for eight bars if it was available. This was another point which could only be fully brought to life in a cathedral setting. When that climax dies down, in the rich glow of a summer sunset, it brings with it the glimpse of the opening of the first movement, and with it a peace that lingers with us for a long time.

III. The Concertos

This talk was recorded for the B.B.C.'s Eastern Service in June 1946.

Formally, both of Elgar's Symphonies carry on the torch of Brahms: indeed, he used the mould of Brahms with no innovations except, in the First, the experiment of treating the utmost opposites in key — A flat and D minor — as if they were closely related, and building the whole Symphony on this dual tonality.

In the Concertos, however, he has made some interesting steps forward. The Violin Concerto, which came two years after the First Symphony, is an extended work playing a good fifty minutes in three large-scale movements with great wealth of material and richness of scoring. The opening *tutti*, as in all classical concertos, pours out in an unbroken stream practically all the themes which are used in the movement and it brings us to the first of Elgar's innovations: instead of introducing the solo with a flourish, or at the top of a climax, he makes him insinuate himself into the middle of the texture, and I well remember the thrill of first hearing the tone of Fritz Kreisler's G string unobtrusively carrying on the line of a descending sequence in this way.

The great movement is built up from here in the usual concerto form: exposition, development and recapitulation, and is about twenty minutes long. Its angry close in B minor is gently followed by the beautiful slow movement in B flat major, an unusual and beautiful contrast.

In the last movement we find Elgar advancing the concerto form with a certain hand and a most poetic touch.

The movement opens stormily and its second theme carries on with somewhat less energy. This is a binary movement like some of Beethoven's finales, so the recapitulation follows the exposition at once without a development. But Elgar then (like Beethoven) follows this with a very large coda and we are surprised at once to hear it start with a quotation from the slow movement. Our thoughts are brought back to the finale, but not for long. We next hear the two notes with which the Concerto began its first movement, the two notes we first heard from the solo violin, and out of this emerges Elgar's most notable contribution to the form of the Concerto, a cadenza of unusual beauty and quality, accompanied by a repeated *pizzicato* of the string orchestra — a sort of thrumming — gently rhapsodising on many of the themes of the whole Concerto, not only of this movement. It builds up (on the figure from the slow movement which we heard when the coda began) to finish in a triumphant blaze and broad restatement of the initial figure of the whole Concerto.

I was privileged when still a student to be the guest at a supper party after the first performance of the Violin Concerto, and I heard Elgar greeting a friend of his, Sir Claude Phillips, Keeper of the Wallace Collection, a distinguished writer on painting, friend of musicians, painters and poets, and, as I myself well know, a good friend to aspiring musicians. Elgar's first words were, 'I hope you think that is a work of art'. Phillips' reply was in no uncertain terms.

The 'Cello Concerto was written eight years after the Second Symphony. The War of 1914 had come between, and the opulent and spacious days of King Edward VII had been left well behind. Further, Edward Elgar had written his three notable contributions to chamber music, and particularly in the Violin Sonata a new note of phantasy, of freedom, and of economy, had come into his work. For this reason perhaps the 'Cello Concerto puzzled its hearers at first, and took longer to be understood. The sketches for the unfinished Third Symphony show this new quality again, and we can tell what we have alas lost in having been deprived of this work by the composer's death.

The 'Cello Concerto is in four movements and lasts under half an hour. A hide-bound classicist might say it was not a concerto at all. In that case it is one of the loveliest suites ever written, but we need not quarrel about its name.

The opening of the Concerto forms a link with the whimsical scherzo movement which comes second, and after several false starts finally begins its light-hearted course. Sir Donald Tovey thus sums up this movement: 'Having produced just enough effect of development to take us beyond lyric forms, the impish little movement scurries back to its G major and vanishes with the detonation of a burst bubble'.[1]

I sometimes think that the slow movement, accompanied as it is by a very small orchestra, and plumbing the depths of human feeling, is another portrait of the composer's wife whose loss he was so soon to mourn. Her acknowledged musical portrait we have, of course, always loved in the first of the *Enigma* Variations. In the last movement, after the introduction and start of the movement proper, comes the magical reference to the mood of the slow movement, suddenly breaking into the tersest possible coda which begins with an echo of the first introduction and fits so well in its economy and power the intense concentration of the whole Concerto.

And so we say au revoir to those two splendid examples of Elgar's work. Noteworthy as developments of concerto form, memorable for the intense beauty of their pattern and colour: and when looked at together, historic landmarks of the years of their appearance, 1910 and 1919, reflecting as does all true art the life and feeling of their times.

IV. *Falstaff*

Like the previous talk, this was recorded in 1946 for broadcast on the B.B.C.'s Eastern Service.

Elgar's *Falstaff* may well prove to be the last of the great tone-poems in the history of music. You may remember how, when *The Dream of Gerontius* was first performed out of England, in Düsseldorf in 1902, Richard Strauss rose to his feet at supper and proposed the toast of the first of the New

1. *op. cit.*, Vol. 3, *Concertos*, O.U.P., London, 1935, p. 202; reprinted in *Concertos and Choral Works*, O.U.P., London, 1981.

English School of Composers; he added privately to Elgar afterwards that he envied him, for he would rather be the first of a new school than the last of an old one, and this charming compliment has now proved itself historically correct.

The question has been asked (and I myself heard it from the lips of Sir Landon Ronald, to whom *Falstaff* is dedicated) whether this work has gone beyond the bounds of what is appropriate, and invaded the province of stage music. It is not for me to answer it, but I will say that *Falstaff* was intensely admired by that great judge of structure and style, Sir Donald Tovey. I will admit that it is one of my hopes that I may one day conduct it in an opera house with its glittering pageantry shown on the stage, for I know it would respond magnificently to this treatment even though it is still symphonic music.

The answer to the question and the justification of the work may perhaps be found in the magnificent character-drawing in *Falstaff*. This is the fundamental purpose of the work, as it is described in the analysis which Elgar himself has written; and this is the thread which runs through the work and unifies it. It is summarised in the first of the four parts into which the work is divided, and which lasts only three minutes in a total of thirty-five. Elgar attached to it the following quotation from Morgan's description of Falstaff: 'in a green old age, mellow, frank, gay, easy, corpulent, loose, unprincipled and luxurious'. This section also includes a statement of the theme associated with Prince Henry. I think we may call this the kernel of the work, though we haven't by any means exhausted the musical or dramatic material. I will now just sketch the scenes which have been chosen by Elgar for illustration because of their direct bearing on the character of Falstaff.

Part II begins with Eastcheap where Falstaff and the Prince are found in the company of 'ostlers, carriers, drawers, merchants, pilgrims and loud robustious women'. Then comes Gadshill; the muffled calls in the dark; the struggle for the 'twice-stolen booty', after which robbers and robbed return again to Eastcheap, when Falstaff falls asleep. In his sleep he dreams of his boyhood as Page to the Duke of Norfolk. This, musically, is the first of two Interludes for small orchestra.

Then comes Part III. Falstaff is awake and hurrying off to battle with his 'scarecrow army'. The battle over, the Second Interlude shows Falstaff visiting Master Robert Shallow in his orchard in Gloucestershire.

The Interlude is interrupted by the news that Prince Henry is' now King Henry V, and Falstaff hurries back to London in hopes of royal favours.

Part IV describes his disappointment, decline and death. We start with the King's march, 'glittering in golden coat and gorgeous as the sun at midsummer'. Falstaff approaches the procession, is rebuffed by the King, who rides on, having looked 'on his ancient friend for the last time'. In the closing scene, with Falstaff lying as 'he played with flowers and babbled of green fields', we hear the theme of the gracious Prince Hal; then the nerveless final struggle and collapse; 'the brass,' in Elgar's words, 'holds *pianissimo* a full chord of C major, and Falstaff is dead'. Thus ends Elgar's *Falstaff*.

I heard its first performance at Leeds Festival in 1913 (and remember seeing Arthur Nikisch, who gave many memorable performances at that Festival, sitting eagerly in the front row with a copy of the score), and I see now how significant that date has become, for the catastrophe which began a year later has changed men's thoughts in many ways. We now want our music shorter and more terse; we seem to need a sharper difference in style between the dramatic and the symphonic; and our composers usually write for smaller orchestras and on a smaller scale. Elgar understood this himself, and the few works he wrote after 1914 look forward to the new age, and he himself, like his followers and admirers, said goodbye to the Edwardian style of opulence and magnificence.

V. 'Land of Hope and Glory'

This talk was broadcast on Sunday, 23 February 1941, on the B.B.C.'s Home Service.

I want to talk to you about a tune that is the property of Everyman: 'Land of Hope and Glory'. It comes in appropriately this morning because its composer, Edward Elgar,

died seven years ago today. It is a tune that has won its way
into the hearts of us all, in spite of an occasional sniff from a
highbrow, and it is a tune that I for one would be very proud
indeed to have composed. It is curious, too, that the tune that
we know so well as a song began its life as an instrumental
melody; for it was first heard as the central theme or trio of the
Pomp and Circumstance March No. 1. This kind of change is rare
in modern music; we know how Bach would take a cantata
that he had written for somebody's wedding or birthday and
re-hash it to celebrate the coronation of an elector of Saxony,
or possibly the other way round; but it is unusual to think that
a composer like Elgar should have written a fine march tune
and then, a few years later, been able to adapt it to a poem
which was written for a special occasion.

It is interesting too that there was an idea of making the
great tune fit another poem to suit the mood of 1914. Mrs.
Elgar Blake, the composer's daughter, has let me see some
very interesting letters between composer and poet, discussing
these new verses.

But may I tell you how I came to know it? As a boy on
Sunday afternoons I went as my regular habit during the
winter months to Sir Henry Wood's Queen's Hall Sunday
Concerts. It was the high spot of my school week when I
climbed the steps of the balcony door of Queen's Hall at three
o'clock every Sunday armed with my season ticket. I was at
school at Westminster, and as a boy of thirteen had been
thrilled by the prospect of King Edward VII's coronation in
the summer of 1902. Some of you will remember the shock of
his sudden illness; and when we ought to have been attending
the coronation the boys of Westminster were privileged to
attend an Intercession Service at St. Margaret's with the
members of both Houses of Parliament. Many other things
were cancelled at that time, notably a gala performance at
Covent Garden when Elgar's *Coronation Ode*, written to a poem
by A.C. Benson, was to have had its first performance. This
had to take place later at the Sheffield Festival, and it was
repeated soon after at a Queen's Hall Sunday Concert. It was
not often that we had a choir there and this in itself was a
thrill, as was the engagement at one of our concerts of Dr.
Elgar, as he then was, to conduct, as well as our beloved Mr.

Henry J. Wood and such soloists as Agnes Nicolls, Edna Thornton, Lloyd Chandos and David Ffrangcon-Davies.

'Land of Hope and Glory' is the final number of the *Coronation Ode*, and it begins as a contralto solo, finishing with soloists and chorus in unison backed by the orchestra and organ. The effect was tremendous, and after many recalls Mr. Robert Newman came on the platform and said that he had persuaded Dr. Elgar to conduct the final number again. I think this was the only encore I ever heard at those concerts.

Now let's look at the tune, and hold it up to the light. Why does it mean so much more to us than many another? Have you ever examined its contour and noticed how aptly it contains the two qualities of movement by step with an occasional very telling jump? You see how the first two lines are based on a downward scale, and then we start again upwards. Then the fifth and sixth lines of the poem repeat the music of the first and second as in so many hymns. The seventh and eighth are further followed by a ninth and tenth of similar shape, which prevent the balance of the whole thing becoming too four-square. I think it is this firm framework of slowly moving scale that makes for the permanency of this tune. And if you listen to the rest of the March, you will notice these same characteristics, particularly this scale movement by step, up and down.

'Land of Hope and Glory' has often been called another national anthem, and I can recall a thrilling moment one day at a political meeting in the great Massey Hall, Toronto, when an enormous audience, one and all, took up the tune as an old friend, and joined in with it, following the lead of Dame Clara Butt, who happened to be in the audience and was called up to sing to us. It is a tune that is indeed the property of Everyman.

VI. Elgar as Conductor

This talk was given on the Third Programme in March 1963.

It still seems to be the fashion to say that Edward Elgar was a bad conductor. One can agree that he was not as good as Toscanini or Bruno Walter, but he had other things to do.

When I hear the old remark made by someone who remem-
bers, I like to retort with the following question: 'Have you
ever heard a performance of an Elgar work which has moved
or impressed you more than that work has done when you
heard Elgar himself conducting it?' The answer is always,
'No, I don't think I have'.

This admission is something that applies to very few
composers. Strauss, Weingartner, and, I suppose, Mahler
(whom I greatly regret never to have heard) were, I suppose,
the only exceptions; they were in the front rank of conductors;
they held important conducting posts first, and composed, at
any rate in early life, only in their spare time. Many other
composers have given fairly adequate performances of their
own works, but have almost always failed to get the emotional
proportions right; they start with too much excitement, and
the climaxes are usually misplaced. This aspect of performance — the reproduction of a masterpiece in its true proportions — is, I feel, the hallmark of only the greatest interpreters.

The current number of the journal of the British Institute
of Recorded Sound[1] has a most interesting account of Elgar
the conductor, as seen in his recordings, by Dr. Jerrold
Northrop Moore, who is the Curator of Sound Recordings at
Yale University. Dr. Moore has had access to many unpub-
lished takes which have been preserved from Elgar's recording
sessions, and has studied and listed them all with wonderful
thoroughness.

He relates the story of a performance of *The Kingdom* at
Worcester at which I was present. The choir sang rather out
of tune early in the work, which caused Elgar to lose interest,
and start driving the work through as quickly as possible,
obviously wanting to hear nothing till the last chord. He had
reckoned without his soprano solo, Agnes Nicholls, who had a
quite peculiar reverence for her big aria in the Fourth Scene,
which she knew was written for her. She always said she knew
nothing when she sang the aria; she just shut her book and
gave herself to the music. The moment she started I felt the

1. 'Elgar and the Age of Performance', *Recorded Sound*, Vol. 2, No. 9,
January 1963, pp. 1–7.

orchestra sitting up and recovering their interest, and this soon affected the composer, who seemed to wake up and to resume control, with the result that the rest of the performance was as fine as we could wish.

Elgar conducted other people's music as well as his own only for a short period in middle life, when he was engaged to conduct a tour and a whole season by the London Symphony Orchestra. He was the chief conductor for the L.S.O. in 1912. But it was not a great success, and didn't last very long. It was chiefly as a conductor of his own music that he is remembered.

Finally, I should like to quote Dr. Moore's own words: 'Elgar's interpretations of his works have in common a romantic fervour and a tremendous spirit of artistic conviction, together with what I have heard described as a certain "downrightness" in the total approach. Such qualities as these undoubtedly proceed at least in part from the fact that Elgar was absolutely sure of himself as a conductor of his own works, and in the recording studio he was in his element. He never tried to disguise the fact that his own music thrilled and delighted him.'

HOLST AND DELIUS

Sir Adrian contributed this talk to the Third Programme's *Music Magazine* in March 1963.

Soon after the first (invitation) performance of *The Planets* in the autumn of 1918, several of the Royal Philharmonic Directors (who had been at this performance) asked me whether I would accept an engagement to conduct the work again, at one of two concerts in early 1919, and my friend Geoffrey Toye was also to conduct two. The difficulties of getting a choir for 'Neptune' caused its omission, and also 'Venus', which was thought to be rather more 'ordinary' than the others.

We had the first performance of the Delius Violin Concerto at the other concert, and as the composer was living in London then, we had a good many rehearsals at his home. At one of the last of them we were all horrified to learn that Albert Sammons, who was still in the Guards' Band, had been detailed for duty all night at a Royal Albert Hall Victory Ball on the very night before this important première. Delius nearly went mad, and of course couldn't understand at all that in the England of 1919 a concert was of quite secondary importance to a grand ball at which, I think, royalty was to be present. We all felt powerless until, some hours later, I remembered that I knew that one of the royal Ladies-in-Waiting was fond of music, and I had actually had the honour of meeting her. So I thereupon telephoned to Sandringham, and I believe that a word to Albert's Colonel did the trick, and overweighed the jealousy of his bandmaster, who, it was said, had greatly enjoyed refusing leave to the upstart bandsman.

I had the privilege of fairly frequent appearances with the Royal Philharmonic Society at this time, but I remember most vividly a concert at which I was a member of the audience; in March 1920 when *The Hymn of Jesus* had its first performance, sung by the newly-formed Philharmonic Choir, conducted by Holst himself. It made an unusually profound impression, and I went to the artists' room in the interval which followed, and found half-a-dozen well known London musicians urging the directors to alter the programme of the second half of the concert, and insert an immediate repetition of the Holst work. This was considered impossible — I believe we in England do stick to our printed programmes more than many other people — but an extra concert was arranged for this a month or two later.

LEHÁR

This short reminiscence appeared in a programme called
'Song of Vienna', broadcast on the B.B.C.'s Light Programme
in April 1952.

I left Vienna without seeing anything of Lehár, which was
disappointing, but I knew he was old and not well, and I
thought probably he didn't particularly want to meet me. The
funny thing was that somebody told me he was sure he had
seen Lehár just outside the artists' room after our concert, but
I knew I had seen nothing of him, and didn't even know he
was at the concert.

Then when I was back in London I got a most charming
letter from him. He said how much he admired the playing of
the orchestra, and he had come round to the artists' room
hoping to meet me, but seeing how crowded it was and how
busy I must be, he did not want to bother me so he just melted
away. It never seemed to occur to him that I might really
want to meet him.

RACHMANINOV

Sir Adrian broadcast this tribute to Rachmaninov on the
B.B.C.'s External Service on the evening of the composer's
death on 28 March 1943.

Rachmaninov was a great man. His commanding height, and
slow and majestic way of speaking made a strong impression
on anyone who met him, and a talk with him was a stimulating experience as his cynical sense of humour, and delight in
the droll and in the macabre, were never far away.

As a pianist he stood in the very front rank, and many
able critics would say that he was the greatest of his time.

His compositions were all written with masterly command of means, and a delight in beauty of sound which brings
some of them very near greatness. He might be called the last
of the romantics for his work was European rather than

Russian, and though he sometimes used folk material, his style was that of Tchaikovsky rather than of Mussorgsky.

His death will close the chapter of pre-revolutionary Russian musical history, and his many English friends will mourn the passing of a great figure.

RAVEL

This, too, was a broadcast tribute on the night of the composer's death on 28 December 1937.

Ravel's music, from his youngest days, showed the flavour and style that were also associated with his maturity. Chiefly a miniaturist, he could, however, fill a large canvas well and with a fine grasp of structure. He knew exactly when to stop, as is seen particularly in his well-known *Bolero*, where the art of orchestral crescendo is shown off with an almost aggressive brilliance until just one moment before the hearer must either collapse from excitement or explode from irritation.

Many of his songs and pianoforte pieces are well-known, and he could claim our own Vaughan Williams as a pupil, although his influence on him is not especially remarkable. Together with Debussy, though in quite a different way, he broke the ice which was forming over French music as the followers of Franck and Saint-Saëns settled into their styles, and his progressive influence was felt far beyond his own country.

Ravel made many friends, and his visits to England — all too rare — were events which will not be easily forgotten. I remember in particular what was probably his last visit when he came to the Royal College of Music and heard us giving a rather ill-rehearsed account of the closing scene from *Daphnis and Chloë*. He was charming about it, and even helpfully went into details about our performance, and actually corrected a couple of misprints in our copy of the score.

Of his orchestral works, after *Bolero*, perhaps the *Mother Goose* Suite and the *Tombeau de Couperin* are best known, but it is his biggest — and, I think, his greatest — work, the neglected ballet *Daphnis and Chloë*, that calls out for a full stage performance as a memorial to him.

A lovable creature, he was known often to give a helping hand to younger musicians. His death will be mourned all over the musical world, and his work will live after him for many years.

SCHUBERT

Symphony No. 9 in C major

This is the text of an interval talk given on the Home Service in December 1943.

Now we come to one of the grandest symphonies in the whole of music — Schubert's 'Great C major'. Most of you know it well already, I expect, and find that every time you hear it, fresh beauties are seen and its greatness seems greater still. It may be new or nearly new to some of you and I would suggest that those newcomers should first remember that it lasts nearly an hour and so each of its four movements will fill a wider space than we are accustomed to expect. Let's prepare for great, bold sweeps of colour and let the stately drama unfold itself at its leisure. The first movement opens with a spacious introduction. The horns display its theme without accompaniment:

Andante

This is repeated several times with increasing power. After four or five minutes, the excitement grows and the full orchestra leads us on into the movement proper, which is based on this insistent, masculine theme:

It's interesting to note that its first form was this:

and Schubert only made the alteration after the score was finished. Sir Donald Tovey has counted several hundred of these alterations, laboriously done with a penknife.[1] The far stronger, second thought is never far away right through the movement. It unfolds a scheme of dignity and firmness. There's a long passage of mystery which I'll speak of again later, about two-thirds of the way through and from here on it builds up to its close, which involves a sudden quickening of pulse and then a slow-down and a restatement of the horn theme of the introduction, rounding off the movement with strength and dignity.

The second movement follows in a minor key. Now some people see nothing in this movement but light-heartedness, perhaps children's play. They feel that the pace in many performances is too slow for them. Well, I think I differ. There's surely something wistful in that opening tune of the oboe, joined later by the clarinet:

 etc.

I see in this a contrast to the forthright optimism of the first movement. Surely that opening, if played more briskly and with no shadow to it, takes away all or most of the meaning from the calm and comforting second violin theme which follows:

 etc.

1. *op. cit.*, Vol. 1, *Symphonies 1*, O.U.P., London, 1935, pp. 205–211; reprinted in *Symphonies and Other Orchestral Works*, O.U.P., London, 1981.

And then, too, that moving scene from another world, where the horn repeats a bell-like note against a wonderful progression of string chords, leading back to our first oboe theme. And again, without a note of the wistfulness in that opening: what can that shattering catastrophe mean, fairly late on in the movement? Surely such a storm couldn't come out of a cloudless sky? The silence that follows it, and that amazing answer from the 'cellos, lead us again to the calm and comfort of the second theme, and so to the close, with another extended reference to our wistful opening.

The third movement is a scherzo, as evolved by Beethoven out of Haydn's minuets; it rings along with real Viennese fun, and the opening figure is tossed about the orchestra with fascinating good humour. The alternative trio comes in a smoother mood. Perhaps the dancers are sitting out to one of Schubert's endlessly beautiful melodies, but the scherzo returns, of course, and is re-played again in a shorter form.

The fourth movement is, as Sir Donald Tovey points out,[2] a rare instance of a completely successful last movement of Schubert. He gathers up the moods of the three acts of the drama that are past, and after an opening that is so original that the violins both in Vienna and London seriously jibbed at it when first asked to play it, he rolls us along with an irresistible dash and speed until, in a couple of minutes, we are brought up short with a crash and a moment's silence. Then follows, quietly at first, a tune, a great tune, built on four repeated notes:

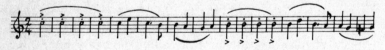

As it grows in stature with superb directness and sincerity, it puts me in mind of some devout crusading knight in shining armour, whose power for good grows and grows as the movement develops, and finally, in the closing coda, after a long growing crescendo, built on the four repeated notes, we find them thundered out by all the strings in unison, and evil

2. *ibid.*

disappears from the scene in a triumph of purest right. So far, I have given you just the dramatic basis of the Symphony as I see it, and I would suggest that this is the first thing to listen for in any work by Beethoven or Schubert, or anyone since. But there's something else that I'd like to outline, perhaps particularly for those who already know the Symphony, and that is the structural basis, for music, as I expect you all know, is not just a stream of sound. It is a piece of architecture built up both in its organisation of subjects and in its organisation of keys. Now, in every classical movement, there's a point between halfway and two-thirds of the way through, when we realise that we're in sight of home; the material of the opening of the piece re-appears, and we see the end of our journey coming into view. This point is also an emotional and dramatic highspot in the movement. The mood may be fierce in its intensity, it may be calm in its mystery, but it underlines emotionally the point of this structural kernel of the movement. From then on, we go over ground that is no longer new to us; we hear tunes we've heard before, in a key which gives us a sense of rest, as a contrast to our previous wanderings.

Let's look at this cardinal point of return in each of the four movements of the Schubert Symphony. First comes the long diminuendo, with snatches of figures that we know, dying down and down until the lowest level of orchestral tone is reached — and mysteriously, in the dim distance, that view of home comes to us, and we realise that the insistent masculine theme of the opening is with us again. In the second movement the unearthly beauty of the alternation of the bell-like horn note and strong chords lead us back to our first wistful oboe tune. And in the third movement the last part of the trio, smooth and melodious, is followed by some repeated notes which get more and more insistent until they foreshadow the brisk, good-humoured swing of the opening of the Scherzo. Finally, in the fourth movement we hear those four repeated notes everywhere. Our knight in armour is growing in stature, the music drops down to the bass as if crouching before a spring. Suddenly there's a blinding flash and we think of the abrupt opening of the movement. The key is E flat which gives us added brilliance, but our whirling movement is again under way and it'll swing us round to the C major we're

waiting for in time for the next appearance of the knight and
his four notes.

SCHUMANN

Sir Adrian wrote this essay as sleeve-notes for his recordings of
the Schumann Symphonies on the Pye-Nixa label in August
1956, one hundred years and a month after the composer's
death.

I am very glad to have had the opportunity of recording all the
Schumann Symphonies, because, as a young man, I had some
special opportunities to learn them and to enjoy them. Clara
Schumann, the composer's widow, who long survived him,
was a frequent visitor to England, and many of her pupils and
friends were in London when I first went there. The most
famous of those was Fanny Davies, who carried the Clara
Schumann tradition on for many years and handed it to many
pupils at the Royal College of Music, where I was her
colleague in the early 'twenties. The Director of the College,
Sir Hugh Allen, sent me one evening to discuss some matters
with her, and after we had done our business I took the
opportunity of asking her some questions, notably about the
right treatment of the last movement of the C major Symphony, and how far one should add dynamic marks to the
rather scanty directions left by Schumann. 'Come on, we'll
play it as a duet!' was her answer, and before we were much
older we had played all four Symphonies, and I had had a
wonderful lesson in interpretation. After this, at 1.30 a.m., she
produced a modern Czech symphony, but I felt I couldn't
break the spell of Schumann which she had so magically
called up, and escaped to bed!

There were devoted Schumann-ites in London at that
time who felt that Arthur Nikisch took unwarrantable liberties
with his music, but though Nikisch's performances were
always highly personal, many of us could feel quite happy
when the composer was Schumann. Nikisch himself told how
in the Leipzig Gewandhaus when he was conducting the

Fourth Symphony with Frau Schumann in the audience, he came to the point in the development of the first movement where he usually allowed himself to coax a big *largamente* from the trombones as they lifted the orchestra over a series of beautiful modulations. This had aroused some adverse criticism from the conservatives of Leipzig, and so he ventured a glance to the front row where the old lady was sitting, and was delighted to see her smiling with pleasure.

This Symphony was not Schumann's last, and as great a critic as Tovey considers that the scoring of the final revision is not satisfactory, and an earlier version (which was published fifty years later) is in many ways to be preferred. I myself find the whole work most lovely, and intensely exciting. It follows the usual plan, with a slow introduction to the first movement, an unusual partnership of oboe and solo 'cello in the *Romanze* (with a beautiful violin solo as trio), a vigorous scherzo, and a noble bridge passage leading into the finale, which is built on a major version of the main first movement figure. It is notable that Schumann does not close any movement finally, but carries the signature on to the next movement, indicating that there should be no break in the performance of the Symphony as a whole.

The First Symphony is sometimes called *Spring*. It comes from the happiest time of his life when he was married to the ideally sympathetic and musical lady who, as we have seen, was an artist and teacher whose influence helped hundreds of later interpreters. In each movement he pours out a stream of lovely lyricism, and even Tovey (whose impatience with Schumann's scoring is only matched by his delight in his sense of beauty) felt that the orchestration here is generally adequate.

The Second Symphony in C major is a bright and dramatic work, and it was its last movement, which looks, on paper, like a rather soulless procession of a somewhat aggravating one-bar figure with no particular rhyme or reason about it, about which I questioned Miss Fanny Davies. Her answer was gloriously convincing: she played no two bars alike; the figure sprang to life, and above all became part of a sweeping line with a wealth of rhyme and reason urging it on. The other movements play themselves more easily, the first throwing a strong accent on to the second beat of many of its ¾ bars, the second a real scherzo in ²⁄₄ time racing on with its ceaseless semi-quavers until it exhausts the performer even if it exhilarates the listener, and the third, one of Schumann's finest lyrics.

The Third Symphony is in E flat, with five movements. The first, in ¾, was thought by Sir Donald Tovey to owe some allegiance to the *Eroica*. I feel it, somehow, brisker and busier than Beethoven's great *Allegro*, though full of life and high spirits; it is followed by a charming *Ländler* type of movement in which Tovey found a Rhenish flavour. The slow movement has some lovely Schumann tunes. The noble fourth movement, said to depict the emotions of anyone looking at Cologne Cathedral, has, with the *Ländler*, no doubt given the unofficial title of *Rhenish* to the whole Symphony. It certainly seems right that we should look on this so-called fourth movement as a slow introduction to the lively finale, at the exciting end of which its material finally re-appears to give it a most convincing peroration.

Those who buy these records may perhaps be interested by a word or two on Schumann's scoring. Authorities always underline his weakness in this respect, but Tovey considered his early works show a better orchestral sense than later, when he had had the experience of holding the position of conductor at Düsseldorf. His diffidence, and one or two early shocks, started him playing for safety, especially in the woodwind department. Where he formerly would have entrusted a tune to one soloist, he later became frightened, and for safety would give it to three or four, resulting in a thick and colourless unison. Several great conductors have issued amended editions; in my opinion they go unnecessarily far, and the present performances preserve, in general, Schumann's own scoring. Where Schumann's safety measures have produced a disagreeable thickness, we have sometimes cut out these doublings, of course without losing any of the harmony notes, and in other places we have reduced the dynamic markings of Schumann's accompaniments in order that his exquisite tunes may be fully enjoyed. By these occasional amendments we hope that the full beauty of these lovely works can be realised.

SIBELIUS

This birthday message to Sibelius on his seventy-fifth birthday
on 8 December 1940 was broadcast in the 9 p.m. news
summary.

It is my very great privilege and pleasure to send to Sibelius
on his 75th birthday affectionate good wishes and congratula-
tions on behalf of all musicians and music lovers throughout
the British Empire. I am delighted, too, to be able to tell him
that, beginning on the 20th December, the B.B.C. is going to
broadcast all his Symphonies (one in each week) and I am
proud to have the honour of conducting the First Symphony
myself.

I can assure Sibelius that it is gratifying to us to be able to
pay a tribute which gives such deep pleasure, not only to those
who already know and love his music, but especially to those
who have the honour to perform it.

ETHEL SMYTH

These reminiscences were written in November 1956 for
Christopher St. John, whose book *Ethel Smyth* (now out of print)
was published by Longmans in 1959.

I knew some of Dame Ethel's music as a young man, and I
remember her taking a call when Nikisch did *The Cliffs of
Cornwall* at a very early London Symphony Orchestra concert,
but when I went (in 1921, I should think) to the Munich
Festival with a letter of introduction from Robin Legge to
Bruno Walter, he asked after Dame Ethel and was astonished
that I didn't know her. I had to explain that I was brought up
in Liverpool, and didn't know many people in the musical
world.

When Sir Henry Wood resigned from the Birmingham
Festival Choral Society in 1923, he had already made plans
for the 1923–4 season, and I was happy to take on the
programmes, including Ethel Smyth's Mass, which was a

revival after thirty years' neglect. We had many talks
together, at Woking, in London (where I then lived), and also
for an intensive weekend at Hill Hall in Essex, where, besides
Mrs. Charles Hunter, who looked most impressive sitting at
the head of the table with her Sargent portrait on the wall
behind her, there was another sister with a daughter, and
together I found the conversation much more than entertaining! I remember a shock at Liverpool Street when we were
going down there. Dame Ethel had a bad cold, produced from
her pocket a large roll of paper with perforations clearly
showing, and blew her nose on a portion which she then threw
out of the window. She was always ahead of her time — I
suppose Kleenex didn't come for twenty years after that!

We worked hard at Hill; every nuance was discussed, and
I think we took turns at the piano but both sang, or rather
howled, most of the time. I believe that I had a postcard every
second day from then on to the date of the performance. I am
sorry I didn't keep them.

The following year I took on the Birmingham City
Orchestra, and saw little of friends in London, though I think
Dame Ethel came down once or twice when I did *The
Boatswain's Mate* Overture or the *Interlinked Melodies*. We also
met over a performance of *Fête Galante* in Bristol.

It was in 1929, I think, that her old friend Jack Somer-
ville (the most go-ahead Commandant the Royal School of
Military Music has ever known) invited me to take over the
London Bach Choir of which he was Chairman. I suggested
The Prison, and I remember seeing Mrs. Hunter always sitting
at the back for the weekly rehearsals, even when Dame Ethel
wasn't there. We also began then the annual complete
performance of the Bach *St. Matthew Passion*, and it was in
1931, I believe, that I conducted it for the last time, as B.B.C.
work made everything else impossible.

VAUGHAN WILLIAMS
I. R.V.W. at 75

Sir Adrian recorded this assessment of Vaughan Williams for
the B.B.C.'s European Service in September 1947. It was
broadcast to mark his seventy-fifth birthday on 12 October
1947.

In these disturbed times it is natural that the thought of
leadership should be constantly in men's minds. It all matters
very much indeed, and the whole question of leadership, and
its transference, is in constant discussion. So it is refreshing to
turn to a world where leadership is undisputed, and hardly
ever mentioned, where, in fact, several leaders could be
tolerated at once, each going his own way undisturbed by the
others. Yet in this world (I refer, of course, to the world of
musical composition) my memory brings back a picture of
undisputed leadership in nearly every country for most of my
life.

As a young man in Germany Richard Strauss was
already the leader and the doyen of composers. In Paris
Camille Saint-Saëns, Gabriel Fauré and Albert Roussel suc-
cessively held this position by general consent, not necessarily
because their output seemed of permanent importance
(though it usually was), but because, as men, they were
expected and often asked to take the lead in their musical
world, and their wisdom and judgment were respected and
followed by their younger colleagues.

At the present time, though he holds no official position,
Ralph Vaughan Williams is the undisputed leader of English
musical life. I think everyone will agree that his magnificent
output has for the last forty years enriched the whole world of
music, but just as a man, too, we all respect and love him and
we listen to what he says. It is natural that his music is valued
at a different height by different critics, and perhaps the
insular position and attitude of England make all our work
less apt for export. It is indeed probable that there are a
number of his works which no-one could expect a foreigner to
understand unless he already knew some of Vaughan Williams' preceding output, and could thus have some idea of the

development of his, and our, musical language. But there is plenty of it to appeal to every ear, and I have vivid and happy recollections of performances abroad where *Job*, the *Sea* Symphony, the *Pastoral* and F minor Symphonies, and, of course, the *Tallis Fantasia* have been eagerly rehearsed by foreign orchestras, and equally eagerly welcomed by their audiences.

It has become the custom to divide a composer's work into three periods, and, as a general rule, this does serve to give a rough guide to the development of his mind and his music. But I very much wonder if I could draw any satisfactory lines of demarcation in the case of Vaughan Williams. The difficulty in making any kind of division or classification of Vaughan Williams' output is mainly due to the amazing diversity and pace of development from work to work. Rather than three periods one could place each and every work in a separate category, because, while still unmistakably Vaughan Williams, it shows a marked maturity over its immediate predecessor. Here he differs greatly from his contemporary Arnold Bax, whose style is unified to such a degree that if, say, any of his Symphonies had been published out of its chronological place, this might easily remain undiscovered by critics.

As a young man Vaughan Williams was naturally intensely interested in the recent discoveries of English folksong by Cecil Sharp and others, and he himself is responsible for writing down a number of these direct from the lips of village singers. He has edited a number of them with pianoforte accompaniments, and their style, in particular their modal scales, has naturally influenced his early work. With *Greensleeves*, for example, the magnificent tune in the Dorian mode is something that has become a part of Vaughan Williams himself.

But when you compare the comparative simplicity of his early tunes, such as the song, *Silent Noon*, or his hymn-tune setting, *For All the Saints*, with his first important work for orchestra without chorus the *London* Symphony, or 'Symphony by a Londoner', written when he was forty, you will see how his tunes have matured. Before he had written the *London* Symphony he had the experience of a number of extended works for chorus and orchestra behind him, and one can already see a certainty of touch about his orchestration, which, I think it may be said, was the side of his work which was slowest to perfect itself. I do not mean by this that he was slow to recognise the quality of instrumental sounds; in fact, his early period gives evidence of an astonishing ability to handle colour in, for example, the song-cycle for tenor, string quartet and piano, *On Wenlock Edge*, set to lyrics from Housman's *A Shropshire Lad*.

Vaughan Williams, like all great artists, is a prophet, and already in 1935 he seemed to get the war 'off his chest' in a fine choral work, *Dona Nobis Pacem*, and his Symphony No. 4 in F minor, the last movement of which is hardly less forbidding than the first: it piles up towards its end, until the composer clears the idea of war from his mind with a magnificent gesture of disgust. And when Europe was plunging into war, Vaughan Williams was looking ahead to the world we hoped would emerge, and his deep study and pre-occupation with Bunyan's *Pilgrim's Progress* gave him material for a wonderful vision of peace and beauty in his Symphony No. 5, in D.

I am proud to say that there are plans for the first performance of a still newer Symphony, which I have been asked to conduct next April. I have already had the privilege of making its acquaintance on paper, and have every confidence that it is another notable development in the composer's work. It is true Vaughan Williams, and it seems to say more, and plunge deeper into those thoughts which take us away from this troubled world to beauty and peace.

II. The *London* Symphony

This talk was given in a concert interval in July 1965.

When I look back on my rather long and, may I say, interesting and very enjoyable musical life, it seems that the development did not come regularly but rather in jerks. And one of these jerks caught me very badly at the age of nineteen when I suddenly realised that there was a whole school of wonderfully fine British music at my disposal. Up to that time I'd been in London at school, at Westminster, and had attended very regularly Sir Henry Wood's wonderful Sunday

Concerts at which he gave us the whole of the standard repertoire of the great classics. True, we always had the *Enigma* Variations once a year, and I had heard one or two performances of *The Dream of Gerontius*. But outside Elgar's hardly any name was familiar to me and when I joined the Oxford Choir at the age of nineteen I suddenly discovered a completely new field under the wing of that wonderfully dynamic musician, Dr. H.P. (later Sir Hugh) Allen.

We began working actually in my first term on Hubert Parry's oratorio, *Job*, a work not very well known now, but I venture to think it will be again. I had the pleasure of conducting it about three years ago, and its splendid dramatic power and wonderful characterisation of words impressed me just as much as it had as a young man. At those Oxford rehearsals I was so bewildered that I couldn't make out whether it was the dynamic personality of Hugh Allen that was impressing me with the greatness of this music rather than the music itself. But as time went on, the music itself gained in stature and I realised that Allen was only, as he should be, the vehicle for it. Well, as soon as we had disposed of the Parry concert we went on with *Toward the Unknown Region* by Vaughan Williams. And to my young mind that was, of course, more difficult to understand. It took me quite a time to appreciate it as music. But Allen's persuasive powers got away with it, sooner or later, and when I was twenty we performed *Toward the Unknown Region* in Oxford, and found it very impressive indeed.

The link with Vaughan Williams became personal. He used to come and stay with Allen, and he came for that performance. I was quite excited when a friend of mine invited me to Yorkshire to stay with him for the Leeds Festival of October 1910, because as well as the first performance of the delightful *Songs of the Fleet* by Stanford we were to have the first performance of Vaughan Williams' *Sea* Symphony. Stanford had been conductor of the Leeds Festival for a good many of the triennial occasions, but this was his last. The *Songs of the Fleet* were beautifully sung by his great friend Harry Plunket Greene, and it was a great occasion. But I think it was a day later when Vaughan Williams, whom I had got to know by that time, came to conduct the *Sea* Symphony. This did really strike a startling new note in the whole of the English musical world. In those days the Leeds Festival employed an orchestra chosen from the very finest players in the land and, in fact, it consisted of many of the people whom one saw in the summer at Covent Garden, and who by that time had formed the London Symphony Orchestra which had a tremendous reputation, being conducted by all the greatest conductors from abroad, as well as Hans Richter, in particular, in this country.

As I say, the *Sea* Symphony made a tremendous impression. Hugh Allen came to the performance, and nothing would then do but that the Oxford Bach Choir had to give the second performance in the following March under the direction of the composer. We worked very hard at it. I was privileged to work not only as a singer in the chorus, but also at the orchestral rehearsals. Allen used to train his own orchestra, which at that time could support a pretty good symphony concert with only a half a dozen or so professionals from London — otherwise they were complete on their own. Of course, the Vaughan Williams was extremely hard and they had to do a lot of preliminary rehearsal work. I would be there with a score ready to fill in any gaps for any of the intruments who weren't there — I was always at the piano at those orchestral rehearsals.

It has been said very often that Vaughan Williams was a person who learned the hard way. He didn't have the gift of scoring, of writing for instruments in the way his friend and colleague Holst had, for instance. I remember in Oxford a week or two before the orchestra took on serious study of the *Sea* Symphony, the leader of the orchestra, a very able violinist named Mary Venables, who was known to Oxford audiences through a long series of years, and Vaughan Williams and Hugh Allen spent the whole day at Allen's house going through the string parts of the *Sea* Symphony and making them, well, playable. They were almost unplayable at Leeds and it was only that brilliant orchestra that could make a show of playing some of the extraordinarily intricate and difficult passages; and so the work was considerably simplified ready for the second performance. He altered a certain amount of the choral work, too. I have my original score which shows quite a number of different things, again through

simplification. Vaughan Williams, already in those early days
but as he went on, too, always used an India rubber considerably more than a pencil. And his simplifications had a great
deal to do with the greatness of his music.

The *Sea* Symphony had thus been performed twice, and it
was repeated again a couple of years later at Oxford, so I
knew it pretty well before the 1914 War had started. But
during the War music was, of course, held up. And by 1918 I
had been working, curiously, in the War Office, Leather
Department, and I believe I can claim to have been the first
personal assistant that the man better known as Lord
Woolton[1] ever employed. (He was then a young man from
Liverpool, a friend, and he asked me to go in as his personal
assistant to work at Boots and Leather.)

I had the privilege of conducting a few concerts with the
London Symphony Orchestra at just about the end of the
War. As things had been pretty unmusical all through the four
years, I thought I would like just to see whether I could get
my hand in, and the London Symphony Orchestra were very
glad to have an engagement or two. We put a good deal of
English music into those programmes, but in particular I felt
that the *London* Symphony must go in. It had been performed
only once in London in March or April, 1914, and the
wonderfully enterprising Sir Dan Godfrey had done it in
Bournemouth once during the War. But otherwise it had had
no performances at all. And this, in 1918, was its second
performance in London.

There was a strange history about the score of the work.
Just before the War broke out, after that first March performance which was conducted by Geoffrey Toye, the score was
sent to Germany to be engraved. And it disappeared, and has
never been seen since. I don't know what they did with it, but
it wasn't returned at the end of the war. Anyhow, the score
was needed before that. Luckily the parts were still in this
country and so some of Vaughan Williams' friends took it
upon themselves to reconstruct the score from the parts as

---

1. Born Frederick Marquis, Lord Woolton was Minister of Food, 1940–3,
and Member of the War Cabinet, 1943–5, as Minister of Reconstruction. He
held numerous other appointments.

they went along. The first movement is in the handwriting of
his friend, Professor Edward Dent of Cambridge, and I
believe George Butterworth did one movement before he went
to France, and several other friends were involved in the other
two movements. This score had been bound and was at his
house in Chelsea and so, since he was abroad in the R.A.M.C.
at that time, he told me by letter that the score was available if
I went to Mrs. Vaughan Williams and asked her for it. I took
it out and had the usual struggle that I'm afraid I've always
had on opening a new score by Vaughan Williams. I look at it
for some time and wonder whether I'm ever going to make a
job of it and get to understand it, but somehow or other it
comes in time and one gets command of it. By the time
rehearsals begin one hopes at any rate to be able to guide the
orchestra or chorus concerned and get on with it.

The first performance we gave in that early winter of
1918 was, I think, without the composer's presence, although
I'm not quite sure. There was a frightful air raid that night (at
least, we called it frightful in those days, but 1918 air raids
were not quite as frightful as ones we've come to know since),
enough to keep most people away from the audience, which
was rather smaller than the number of people on the platform.
We had a jolly party in the Queen's Hall cellar afterwards for
quite a time before we were allowed to go home. In view of
that fact I felt it was really up to me to repeat the work a
month later when the final concert of the series was to take
place. I think we took out a Brahms Symphony or something
of the sort and we did the *London* again then.

By now Vaughan Williams had come back to England.
He came to my office, and all among the boots and the leather
samples he sat and revised the score. He was extraordinarily
ruthless about it. In fact, in the third movement there was a
whole third section — one might almost call it the third
subject — which, of course, followed the second subject and
was restated, and there were a good many references to it
during the course of the movement. He cut that and all its
references out ruthlessly. He later had the manuscript score
rebound for me showing all the revisions and it is a wonderfully interesting study for a student of composition. We always
hear it in its revised version today, although some day I hope

the B.B.C. will allow me to do a performance of it in its original form, which takes about seven or eight minutes longer — perhaps a little too long for modern taste.

The *London* Symphony is cast in the usual four movements, the only points about it differing from the classical symphonic mould being that he calls the scherzo a 'nocturne', and that it begins and ends with a Prologue and Epilogue. These were very much extended in the original form. He made them much terser, and the Prologue is now a matter of some two minutes' music, very slow and quiet (here one could apply the title 'nocturne' that he applied to the scherzo). It is a lovely picture of London at night, with an echo of Big Ben. The whole thing builds up gradually, and suddenly, after a moment of silence, we burst into what I can only think of as a vision of Piccadilly at its noisiest and most cheerful. The second subject is obviously a reflection of a cockney mood, and you can almost hear a street boy whistling the tune which comes towards the end of the second subject. The movement goes on with a development in the usual way — a very quiet, long development, a vision perhaps of darkness again; and the recapitulation is fairly regular, finishing with an exciting coda which brings us to a noisy and brilliant conclusion.

The second movement is uniformly quiet, nowhere rising above *forte*, though one can't say there's no passion in it. There's a great deal of very beautiful feeling and although, as I say, I found it a little alarming to start with, when I was working at it amongst my boots, nowadays it seems very beautiful and natural. I notice in my score that I have a note at the beginning of this movement: 'Not too slow. R.V.W.' That is a typical Vaughan Williams remark. He was an extraordinarily humble person and always was rather terrified that people would be bored by his music. And although the slow movement of the *London* Symphony is spacious, it would have to be taken very slowly to be boring.

Another vision of old London that can be heard during the course of this movement is the dear old hansom cab, a curious contraption with the driver at the back on top and just room for two (or sometimes for three small) people sitting just behind the horse; we climbed in and out in a very awkward way. There were only two wheels, rimmed with India rubber so that they were very quiet and all you heard was the horse's hoofs on the hard road and the jingle of the bells they all had, little small bells (not like sleigh bells nor the bells that we hear on cows and sheep in the Alps), which he uses several times during the course of this movement.

The third movement is headed 'Scherzo: *Nocturne*' and is a picture of a very gay night life, not the quiet London of the Prologue and Epilogue. I notice in my score here that I have a note on the top again from R.V.W. 'This must be as quick as possible'. I remember talking about the pace of this movement with Geoffrey Toye who had conducted the first performance. I said that I felt what I was doing was just on the slow side. He said, 'My dear Adrian, you can't help it — the movement won't go any faster, whatever you do with it'. But although modern orchestras can perhaps go a little faster, one doesn't want to go so fast that there's no time to hear the music. It is in the form of a scherzo with two trios, the second of which has a delightful reference to the sort of mouth-organ which was, perhaps, more common in the days of the composition of this Symphony than it is now. After a few bars of mouth-organ comes a tune, a nice, commonplace tune, that you might hear any street urchin whistling on a London evening. There's also a passage a little after that, near the end of the movement, which I remember R.V.W. directed the cornet players to play as if they were outside the pub on a Saturday night. It is interesting that in the Symphony, rather like the French composers, he uses two cornets as well as two trumpets, and displays the rather vulgar colour of the cornet to great advantage in a number of places. The scherzo finishes in a very beautiful, quiet way and we may assume that London has gone to bed and we are back at the London night that we had at the very beginning of the first movement.

The last movement comes in with a really terrifying discord, which we might even say is a bit frightening still. When it was new, when I first looked at it, I wondered whether the composer hadn't made a mistake — but he hadn't, of course. Very soon, after a moment of introduction, we settle down to a quiet march tune, not funereal but solemn. The music livens up later as we come to an *allegro* handled in a normal way, as in most symphonic movements. The march

tune returns, and we have another reference to Big Ben after
the music has died down a bit. Then we have a long Epilogue
which, as I told you, was considerably longer when the
Symphony was new. With the Epilogue, and one or two quite
queer noises, the movement dies right away and he brings us
back to the London at night which we saw at the beginning.

    It is a work that is very near my heart.

III. Talking about R.V.W.

In December 1968 Robert Layton interviewed Sir Adrian
about his recollections of Vaughan Williams and discussed
interpretative problems that arise in the performance of his
music.

RL: Did Vaughan Williams ever talk to you about his
studies with Ravel, or the other French composers? I know
that he expressed his indebtedness in print.

ACB: No, I can't say that I ever discussed that with him,
perhaps because we were always on the performing side and
not so much on the compositional side of the work. Nor did he
discuss his Max Bruch period. Indeed, I think it is more
surprising that he should have gone to Max Bruch than to
Ravel. But no, I don't remember any reference to them in any
of our talks.

RL: Was Vaughan Williams very helpful in offering advice
to conductors of his works?

ACB: Oh, yes. I always like to have the composer about,
particularly if I'm involved in a first performance. And I must
say that, though sometimes they go astray a bit, on the whole
they contribute immensely — even though they perhaps
lengthen the rehearsal sometimes! In fact, the most striking
example I can show of a man being wrong about the
performance of his own work is actually Vaughan Williams in
the *Pastoral* Symphony. When the *Pastoral* Symphony was first
brewing Vaughan Williams used to say, 'Well, I've got a new
tune' (he always called them tunes). 'I've got a new tune and
it's in four movements and they are all slow. I don't think

anybody will like it much.' Well, that was all we heard of the *Pastoral* Symphony for some time until we were finally allowed to see it. We had the luck to be allowed to have the use of the parts and rehearse it two or three times with the Royal College of Music Orchestra before the first public performance. All the time we were rehearsing it (and, of course, I had a bit of time with the score studying it), I had been very much on the slow side, and the composer was continually at my elbow saying, 'You must take it faster' — much faster than I had imagined it. And then I went away to Birmingham and saw very little of my London friends for those six years. Towards the end of that period I was doing a performance of it abroad. Vaughan Williams came up to the rehearsal and, although he didn't say anything about it then, he came up afterwards and said, 'You know, you're doing it terribly fast. Every move-ment's really faster than I want.' So I reminded him of what happened six years before. 'Oh, well,' he said, 'yes, perhaps that is so but, you see, I've conducted it a bit and I've heard it a good deal now since those days. I realise that it isn't so boring to people as I thought it was going to be.' And so I now go back to my original conception of the *Pastoral* Symphony.

RL: In fact, I was going to ask you if you have ever conducted the *Pastoral* Symphony (which is, after all, a very English work) abroad, because I would have thought that this was a very difficult work for a non-English audience to take in.

ACB: Yes, I have. And I think on only two occasions, and both in the same place, the city in Europe which I think is the most avid (in spite of what St. Paul said about Athens) for modern things: Prague. The first performance was at an international contemporary festival, and it made such an impression there that about four years later they asked me to go again and do the same work. Otherwise I don't think I should have been allowed to do the *Pastoral* Symphony abroad, or much in England for that matter. It is the most elusive, isn't it, so that it seldom has performances.

RL: I was very glad to hear a French critic, a great admirer of Vaughan Williams, saying very recently on the Third Programme that this was his favourite of the Symphonies. My

impression is that, apart from Scandinavia, where his Symphonies are given, he is sadly neglected. I wondered if your
impression was similar?

ACB: I don't really know enough to say that. I certainly
think he's not done enough. I've done V.W. abroad. You
mentioned Scandinavia: I did the *Sea* Symphony in Stockholm
a good long time ago. I did *Job* at one festival, and Bruno
Walter came round afterwards with tears in his eyes, and said,
'It's most wonderful music'. And, of course, he was a great
Vaughan Williams enthusiast: he did the Fifth and the Sixth
Symphonies, both in America.

RL: I wanted to put one point to you. I have recently heard
the Fourth Symphony in a performance which perhaps wasn't
terribly persuasive, but it did appear to be one of the works
which didn't seem to wear as well as I'd remembered it. I had
always loved it ten years ago (and perhaps this is a personal
reaction), but I felt that there was something much more
self-conscious in his reaction to the continental scene, both
musically and politically, than there is in, say, the Fifth
Symphony, which always remains fresh to me and grows. I
think this quietest side of Vaughan Williams is the real side.
Do you think this is an unfair reaction?

ACB: No, I don't really. I know people who are tremendous
Vaughan Williams enthusiasts and yet don't like the Fourth
very much at all. Personally (although, of course, nobody
really knows what it is), I always feel that the Fourth, coupled
with *Dona Nobis Pacem*, got the war off his chest. Some other
people think that it was a personal thing, that he realised at
this time that his first wife was not going to get better — she
was very badly crippled with arthritis. Anyhow, he was
getting something evil off his mind. I can quite understand
your finding performances of the Fourth unconvincing if the
dynamics are not watched. The whole of that last movement
can be played at a steady *fortissimo* and it means absolutely
nothing. If people will only look at the dynamics and see
where he has written *forte* and where he has marked *mezzo
forte*, as he does a good way through that movement, it makes
a very different impression.

RL: What sort of impression did the Fourth Symphony make on the audiences of the time?

ACB: The first performance at the Queen's Hall was very, very warmly received. (I think this was the last performance the first Mrs. Vaughan Williams ever heard.) People were puzzled, of course, just as they were by the last movement of the Sixth when it first came out. But I think they accepted it. Then perhaps I'm not the best person to talk about that because I'm amongst his friends, or I've been amongst his friends all the time.

RL: Were you seeing him a great deal?

ACB: On and off, yes, although of course it varied. In the 'thirties, when I was at the B.B.C., I did see a fair amount of him, and we lived not far from them in Surrey. My wife used to go over and see Mrs. Vaughan Williams quite a lot.

RL: I also wanted to ask you whether there are any Vaughan Williams scores that you feel are particularly under-rated nowadays — like the *Concerto Accademico* which I can't remember having heard for years, and which I see from Michael Kennedy's book[1] you recorded with Menuhin. It was never issued.

ACB: I thought it wasn't. We had quite a happy morning with it, but I don't know why they didn't issue it. I don't know the whole range widely enough. I know there are certain works which I should like to hear more; *Dona Nobis Pacem* is one. It's very much neglected, I think.

RL: Is *Flos Campi* another?

ACB: I haven't so much affection for that as for other things, although it is very lovely. And some of the choral work wants doing more than it is.

RL: I know that he had a great admiration for Sibelius and took a great interest in —

ACB: — Everything really.

1. Michael Kennedy, *The Works of Ralph Vaughan Williams*, O.U.P., London, 1964; revised edition, 1980.

RL: I wondered how extensive his interest was in contemporary music on the Continent.

ACB: He knew a great deal that was going on, although he was tremendously interested in young English composers. He was always to be seen at concerts, as you know, avidly drinking up what these young people were doing, whether he liked it or not.

RL: Would you agree that his orchestration was in any sense vulnerable?

ACB: It was to start with, but he was never tired of learning. He was always picking someone's brains, always getting some orchestral player to come and play parts to him, and this kind of thing. He went on learning all his life. As we all know, the violin parts of the *Sea* Symphony were really quite impossible to start with. And he wasn't satisfied with a good deal of his orchestration. He was always asking people's advice, asking them to revise for him. I remember he pointed to a passage very near the end of the first movement of the *London* where the second subject comes on the trombones now. He pointed to it, and said, 'at the first performance, when Geoffrey [Toye] was conducting, I was most disappointed about the effect of that, and Cecil Forsyth was near me. Then not only all the trombones but the string basses were playing the second subject figure for two parts. Cecil said to me, "Cut out the strings". I cut out the strings there and then at the rehearsal, and the trombones alone sounded twice as brilliant.'

RL: Do you in any way feel that there is a falling-off after the Sixth Symphony?

ACB: I wouldn't say falling-off, although, of course, I'm not a critic. All I feel is that the Eighth and Ninth are not so strikingly fresh. There's more of the 'obvious' Vaughan Williams (if we can put it that way) in them than there is in any of the other Symphonies. And of his experiments with the vibraphone and so on: well, he was always after something new — writing tuba concertos and things. It's probably youthfulness, really, one might say: having the fun to explore some quite new thing and make a show of it in a way that's never been done before.

RL: I think that there are some passages in the *Antarctica*, which is underrated, where you feel that he's a prisoner of his own mannerisms, where the modality has become a straight-jacket rather than a natural mode of utterance.

ACB: Yes, I would agree with that to a certain extent. Of course, the *Antarctica* doesn't really rank as a symphony. In fact, I would say that *Job* is really more of a symphony than the *Antarctica*.

RL: The Ninth seems to me to have some very marvellous things.

ACB: I quite agree with you.

RL: I feel that in some ways *Job* is one of his most characteristic and penetrating works. You gave the first performance, didn't you?

ACB: No, not the first performance. The first performance was at the Norwich Festival, as a concert piece (I'm not quite sure, although it's all in Michael Kennedy's book[2]). As a ballet it was not done until later, with Constant Lambert's revised, reduced scoring. As to how it came my way: I was at the B.B.C., so we gave both studio and Queen's Hall performances of it quite soon after the Norwich performance. We had a good deal of trouble because there was quite a demand for it abroad at the time and there was only the one score. It so happened that I had to give up the Bach Choir at that time, and the Bach Choir people were kind enough to want to give me a parting present, so finally, after a good deal of discussion, we decided that an engraved score of *Job* would be a very happy present, and the Bach Choir kindly contributed to give a sum to the Oxford Press for the engraving of the work. I believe that as the royalties come in and the Oxford Press recoups itself, that money is finally to go to the Musicians' Benevolent Fund. Of course, the dedication was a surprise to me, too, because we were still giving performances from this single manuscript score. One day, when he knew what we had done with the Bach Choir, I opened the score to take the

2. *ibid.*

rehearsal, and there at the top of page one were the words 'To Adrian Boult', which touched me immensely. I've been fortunate enough to have a number of very fine works dedicated to me, but I think that really is the one of which I am proudest.

IV. A Tribute

Both Sir Adrian and Vaughan Williams were active in the work of Federal Union, an organisation that worked towards the establishment of a united Europe. Ten days after R.V.W.'s death in August 1958 Sir Adrian wrote the following note for Federal Union's magazine of the same name (which later became *World Affairs* and is now defunct).

The world of music has lost one of its great men — some of us would say its very greatest man — and music in this country is now without the unquestioned leadership which was his. *Musical* leadership implies a restricted field, but it cannot be too often stated that Ralph Vaughan Williams was no ivory tower musician: he gave a valuable and beautiful property to the National Trust; he took an eager hand collecting salvage during the Second World War; he served as an R.A.M.C. orderly in the First when well over age; he was a Vice-President of Federal Union; and some years before 1939, when speaking in public, he expressed a wish to see the United States of Europe.

His interest in Federal Union began in 1940, and he was a prophet in his music as in life; in 1935 his Fourth Symphony in F minor gave a vivid picture of war and its horrors, and its end utters what can only be explained as a fierce gesture of disgust. I hadn't previously felt that music could describe such a thing, but there it is. And in his Fifth he shows us what the world might be if men 'could brothers be', as an apocryphal verse of the National Anthem has it.

He was, like most great men, approachable, sympathetic, and of a piercing integrity. He was to be seen at any concert where an important new work was to be played, and a few hours before his death he was giving advice to a young composer.

He was eighty-five and Mrs. Vaughan Williams tells us that there are practically no unfinished manuscripts: he had completed all the work he had planned, and was ready. But his friends were not; he had become such a tower of strength that one felt he was immortal physically, as indeed he is spiritually.

FRIENDS AND CONTEMPORARIES

Ethel Smyth * Henry Wood
Arthur Nikisch * Gustav Holst
Ralph Vaughan Williams

This talk was broadcast on the B.B.C.'s Home Service in April 1965 in a series entitled *Friends and Contemporaries*.

Whenever I hear *The Wreckers* Overture, by Ethel Smyth, it brings back thoughts of Covent Garden in Edwardian times, and the performances, in German of course, which took place somewhere about 1906, long before I had the great experience of knowing her. This came much later, when in 1924 Sir Henry Wood, resigning from the Birmingham Festival Choral Society, recommended them to appoint me to succeed him, and I found Ethel Smyth's Mass down for performance. It had never been revived since its first performance under Sir Joseph Barnby in 1893. We had a very exciting time with it. It is a very exciting work anyway, with some splendid moments, even though it is rather unequal; but it was thirty-three years old, and Dame Ethel had matured a good deal since it was written, and her ideas about its performance were not, shall we say, quite crystallised. (In fact, I was later reminded by an orchestral player that when she turned up at a rehearsal I greeted her, rather rudely, with 'Good morning, Dame Ethel, and what are your tempi for today?') Anyhow this revival led to others, and I certainly feel Ethel Smyth's Mass might well be heard again from time to time. And her books, too, are still worth reading — she was as good an author as composer.

Although Hans Richter gave me my first experience of an orchestral performance, it was Sir Henry Wood who on most Sundays and many Saturdays when I was between the ages of twelve and nineteen introduced me to the great orchestral repertoire and enabled me to become familiar with the whole field of orchestral music current at that time. He often invited the leading composers of the day, like Strauss and Debussy, to direct their new compositions at his concerts, so we were able to keep abreast of modern developments also. I first met him when his orchestra was engaged to play Holst's *The Planets* for the first time. He came to the rehearsal and performance which I conducted, and was most helpful and friendly to one he might easily have thought of as a tiresome upstart, but I must leave Imogen Holst to tell you below of that eventful day.

As I have said, I owed to Sir Henry my first job in Birmingham when he nominated me as his successor in the direction of the Festival Choral Society. This was my first introduction to the city where I was to spend six very happy years. He was constantly helpful and encouraging to younger musicians; I still have, for instance, in my score of *The Creation* a postcard in his clear, bold writing detailing the exact time taken by each part of it — I imagine I had simply written to ask for this information, and he had personally attended to my query. I remember, too, his surprise when, in my early thirties, I conducted a season for Diaghilev while carrying on with other things instead of resting every afternoon. He strongly advised me to contract the habit of regular rest all the afternoon before any performance, which I did adopt very soon after, and added, characteristically, 'No nonsense on sofas or armchairs; take your clothes off and go to bed'.

It was at the invitation of Sir Henry, in 1902, that Arthur Nikisch came to London for the first time, and made an instant sensation, to be repeated a few years later, when he often came to conduct the London Symphony Orchestra.

Once when Richter and Nikisch gave performances of *The Flying Dutchman* Overture within one week in London, a clever critic said: 'With Nikisch you felt that Fate was pursuing you wherever you went; with Richter Fate was facing you wherever you turned'. This rock-like solidity, and its architectural inevitability seemed even to my immature mind to fit the classical mood more closely. But here is a charming description of Nikisch's imaginative power in rehearsal told by another great artist, Elisabeth Schumann:

> I was sitting in the rehearsal of the Gewandhaus in Leipzig. He had a wonderful orchestra trained by him for years, but suddenly (I think it was in Brahms) he said, 'Gentlemen, it is not beautiful what you do. It is not what I want — play it more "blue".' I thought, 'it is funny, the expression', but it really was a blue sound, and you saw the blue air, you imagined that you saw blue skies.

Nikisch was always a friendly and interested explorer of new movements, and as he came to England every summer for many years, he interested himself in our composers. I remember he made a special journey to London to conduct the first performance of Arthur Somervell's *Thalassa* Symphony; he took charge of a Holbrooke opera; of several Elgar works; and at the Leeds Festival in 1913 I heard him conduct the first performance of George Butterworth's *A Shropshire Lad*. Vaughan Williams and Holst never came his way, I think; he didn't come here after the 1914 War.

Although many of us knew Holst before 1918 it was only a limited number of musicians, and people connected with St. Paul's Girls' School or Morley College, who had begun to appreciate him at his true worth. Vaughan Williams said about his early days:

> In this country our young composers have not those practical opportunities of learning their job as repetiteurs, stage conductors and general assistants in the opera houses and concert rooms. Holst realised this, and partly of course from necessity, but largely from choice, he refused to view the world from the dignified eminence of the organ loft, but rushed into the mêlée of life armed with his trombone, picking up a living where he could, sometimes in a travelling opera company, sometimes playing in a pantomine or the pier band. At one time indeed, he spent his summer dressed up as a Blue Hungarian, where he was admonished with a rude word by the manager to speak

broken English. The result of this unconventional but practical training was that theory and practice always met in him.

Holst worked in Morley College for many years, and organised wonderful things there, as well as taking a body of students down to Thaxted in Essex for week-ends, where they would sing in the church all day and nearly all night; hence the dedication of Vaughan Williams' Mass in G minor 'To Gustav Holst and his Whitsuntide Singers'. They had at Morley a wonderful mock opera with four or five acts, each a parody of some operatic style — Wagner, Balfe, and so on — but I particularly remember the act of Debussy, when on the stage Burne-Jones' grand-daughter sat on the top of a high office stool, and at intervals repeated the words 'I am not happy here' which with considerable skill she sang to the notes of a descending whole-tone scale, a thing I find most difficult to do. Meanwhile Thackeray's grand-daughter, who also was a confirmed Morleyite,[1] walked about the stage very fast for three or four paces and then stopped dead, rather like a guinea pig in a cage. The orchestral accompaniment to all this consisted of fragments of music paper with a phrase of anything from six to twelve bars written on it. Each player had one, and was instructed to start when directed by the conductor and play it over again and again, always as *pianissimo* as possible, until stopped again. The effect was a magical *Pelléas*-like background, and the atmosphere electric!

Holst and Vaughan Williams both had a great sympathy with amateurs — Holst often said: 'If a thing is worth doing at all, it is worth doing badly', and he could be patient with inefficient technique provided it was attached to the right kind of amateur spirit; but, where professional performances were concerned, it was very different and nothing less than the best would do.

I have mentioned the first reading of *The Planets* in 1918 as the event which brought Holst into prominence with a much greater public than before, and here is his daughter Imogen's description of that happy morning:

It was the most wonderful present from his great friend Balfour Gardiner, who was, I think, one of the great patrons of music at

1. 'Morleyite' was Holst's own term for his Morley College pupils.

the beginning of this century. This was at the end of the war in 1918; my father was going out to the Near East to do educational work with the troops, and this was a farewell present.

It was in the Queen's Hall, a private performance, just an invited audience, on one Sunday at the end of September in 1918, and although it's such a long time ago, I can still remember it, some of it very vividly.

Perhaps I may add a personal note to Imogen's description, and the summing-up below by his great friend and contemporary Ralph Vaughan Williams, by telling you that the full score of *The Planets* was beautifully engraved and published quite soon afterwards (in the face of many post-war restrictions and frustrations) and he wrote this charming note on the fly-leaf of my copy: 'This Score is the property of Adrian Boult who first caused *The Planets* to shine in public and thereby earned the gratitude of Gustav Holst'. And let us finish with the appreciation of his friend Vaughan Williams:

If we look at Holst's work as a whole, we find that those delightful tunes which he wrote when he was little more than a boy for children's operas, tinged as they were perhaps with Sullivan and Grieg, are yet the true ancestors of the strong melodies of *The Planets* and *The Perfect Fool* ballet. And in those very same early works we find a hint of what was to develop later into the mysticism of 'Neptune' or the choral song *To the Unknown God* and *The Hymn of Jesus*.

To my mind *The Planets* marks the perfect equilibrium of these two sides of his nature. From the straight-forward tunes of 'Jupiter' — which even those awful people who sing in their baths, would, I believe, manage — down to the strange colours (we can hardly call them harmonies) of 'Neptune', passing through the schoolboy rampage of 'Uranus' with its organ *glissando,* and the ineffable peace of 'Venus': it is all pure Holst.

PART TWO
ON CONDUCTORS

———————————•———————————

TOSCANINI

I. Toscanini's Secret

Sir Adrian broadcast and wrote about Toscanini on several occasions over the many years they were associated. The first of the talks we have selected was broadcast in 1937 and subsequently appeared in *The Listener*.

What is it that makes Toscanini's work so different from that of every other conductor? It is obviously a question that cannot be completely answered, but an attempt may perhaps be made to analyse some of his greatest qualities. The intensity of his power of concentration is certainly what first strikes the listener at one of his rehearsals: it generates such an enormously high voltage of concentration that everyone who comes near is caught up by it and carried along under its spell without a conscious output of effort on his own part. The listener seems to understand and know the music more quickly and more easily than ever before; the orchestra plays the work in a new and different way even at a first reading before the Maestro has explained anything about it. Indeed, so great is the incandescence of this concentration, and so far do it and the irresistible swing of his arm and stick carry one on the road to true interpretation, that the intrusion of verbal explanation (naturally still necessary at certain points) is almost unbearable, and he himself seems to find it so also, for he often forbears to stop the orchestra and carries on, storing the imperfect passages in his memory and dealing with them only after he has played the work to its close.

His wonderful memory is a natural companion to this dynamo of concentration. There are countless stories about it. I think I like best that which tells of the bass clarinet player who came to his room in great trepidation just before an opera performance: a key was broken on his instrument and could not be repaired in time for the show. A few minutes' deep thought (of course, without reference to the score) and the Maestro was telling him how the loss would in most cases be covered by other instruments, but then carefully detailed a few passages where he must arrange for 'cello or bassoon to supply the missing notes. The completeness of the mental picture in sound which emerges from his initial study of a score is shown in others. His sight is so short that he can only see his music when his eye is almost touching the page. It is thus necessary for him to examine the page inch by inch, thereby conveying to his mind an absolutely accurate sound-impression.

Some fifteen years ago when an enterprising impresario made arrangements (which never matured) to bring the Maestro with the Scala Orchestra to London for a series of concerts, he poured out a marvellous series of stories of Toscanini's 'temperament' for the benefit of the more sensational gossip columns. It is natural that one who is endowed with such tremendous vitality and magnetism should have a strong temperament, but nothing that I have ever heard or seen of the Maestro and his work is out of line with a perfectly consistent pursuit of the ideal in music and an absolute horror of personal publicity and showmanship. He cannot be bothered with the second-rate (why should he?), and if people who ought to know better press him to go and conduct orchestras which are quite unworthy of his notice, they have only themselves to blame if after half-an-hour's rehearsal he leaves the hall and takes the next train back to Italy. His sensitivity is such that he modifies his method according to the temperament of the artists he is conducting. Certain nationalities only work their best when driven: these are driven quite mercilessly until they give their best and something more besides. On the other hand, there are those who work best when led; these are led, and the results show the rightness of the method. His whole rehearsal scheme is a model of economy and reasonableness, granted his insistent demand for nothing less than his ideal. He asks beforehand for a generous rehearsal schedule, every minute of which may be used at full pressure if this is necessary to perfect the task he has set himself for the day. If, however, the job is done after one or two hours' work (where three have been planned) the rehearsal is finished, and if he does not need a rehearsal any morning, he cancels it — he will never repeat one bar at rehearsal after he has been once satisfied.

His greatest colleague at Salzburg [Bruno Walter] said to me: 'I never miss his rehearsals; he is like a great high priest of music, caring only for beauty, and the mind of the composer'.

There is not a member of the B.B.C. Orchestra who does not feel immeasurably refreshed and enriched by the experience of these precious weeks of association with one of the greatest interpreters of all time — it comes to an end on the day this appears in print, but all of us welcome this chance of saying: '*A rivederci*, and that right soon'.

II. Toscanini's Musical Fidelity

Broadcast on the B.B.C.'s Empire Service in May 1939.

Toscanini: how can one describe the thrill that belongs to that name? Many of you will have heard his broadcasts — some of you may actually have seen that neat figure, with its splendid head and magnificent dark eyes, sweeping the music from the fingers, lips and hearts of his players and singers. But it is to those who are tonight entering on a new experience that I would like to try and describe the sensations of Toscanini's conducting in the hope that it may make the experience even more thrilling and more lasting. We know that music is the most intangible and fleeting of all the arts, and yet it can provide us with impressions that belong to us permanently just as much as the books and pictures with which we live. And so I find I have a memory that I almost seem to see, of the first concert I heard conducted by the Maestro, and a picture, almost like the vision of a distant mountain range, of the way he heaped climax on climax in the Venusberg music from *Tannhäuser*, each height seeming to call up every ounce of the orchestra's power, only to be succeeded by one more thrilling and more intense.

What are the hallmarks of this intense concentration? First, he will give us every note that the composer has written, every phrase mark, every expression mark, just as it stands in the printed score, in exact proportion, and in such a way that we shall find we hear more than ever before. I don't mean that unimportant instruments will be given undue prominence at unexpected places; it is simply that while we easily follow the *tunes* — the main musical lines at the top or wherever they may be — we shall also hear the secondary lines, as secondary lines, naturally but vitally, where formerly we just heard a background of which we were hardly conscious. What is the cause of this? Well, the Maestro (as we all call him) has a power of absorption far greater than most of us, and he sees with his mind a complete picture of the whole score, where most of us just grasp the prominent part plus a hazy background. The audience hears what the conductor sees, and Toscanini's extraordinarily keen vision enables us to hear far more of the music than ever before.

Besides his faithful reflection of the notes the composer has written, we may expect a warmth and thrill that come to us only rarely in our listening. The actual tone of the instruments seems to be richer and more glowing than usual, and the whole music is conveyed to us with a power and a fire that carry us along, and seem to catch us up with the music, whether we wish it or not. It is impossible to think of anything else while Toscanini is conducting. We are forced to follow and to listen to every detail, as well as to note its flow first to last, and to see the architecture of our music as one great whole.

I said it was impossible to think of anything else while Toscanini conducts. I once tried. An advance copy of a programme had been put into my hand just as he was beginning to rehearse, and I was most anxious to see how a new writer had tackled the problem of analysing a well-known work. I had to give it up, because I couldn't read a sentence without being caught up in the flood of sound that was coming to my ears and wrenched my attention from my reading.

You may have heard that this man of superhuman memory and concentration coupled with a matchless fire and temperament is a trying man to work with and there are stories of the terrible things he has said and done to artists who have incurred his wrath. Well, a master who has for fifty years pursued without flinching the ideal performance, who gives every ounce of his energy for every moment of long rehearsals and performances, who demands the utmost of himself always, is not likely to put up with less than this from the forces he directs. He has an amazing sense of the reaction towards him of the orchestra or choir he is rehearsing, and knows at once whether they too are doing their utmost for the music, or even just a little less, which of course isn't good enough. In this case his tongue is merciless, and his sticks and his music and anything else that is within reach, may find themselves flying through the air or crushed under foot. But if the player is reasonably competent, and obviously trying, the Maestro can be as patient and helpful as anyone. And I do want to rub in how selfless the whole thing is. He is out for a perfect realisation of the music, and everyone is to help in this. The first time I had the honour of introducing him to the B.B.C. Orchestra four years ago, I ventured to outline the history of its association with an increasing number of the greatest conductors, and was just saying that the greatest of all was now with us, when I was interrupted by a hearty thump on the shoulder — 'No, no, no,' he said, 'not the greatest. Just an honest musician, that is all'.

That honesty is linked with a tireless pursuit of the mind of the composer — the slightest detail problem in any work is resolved by reference to some parallel case which shows how the composer's mind was working — or perhaps by reference to the composer's own manuscript if it is available.

Executive artists may be divided into two groups: those who force the attention of the listener on to the music that they are performing; and those who attract that attention on to themselves first, and the music only second; and the greater and more powerful the personality of the artist, the more sharply does it seem to put him into one group or the other. From what I have said you will know that Toscanini most emphatically belongs to the selfless group whose mind is on the composer and on the composer's style and will; who is angry when his own personality is forced into the limelight; whose wish is to be left alone and allowed to be simply 'an honest musician'. He knew, of course, that Beethoven had sent a score of the Ninth Symphony to the Royal Philharmonic Society, and that this score was lent by them to the British Museum. He eagerly asked to see it in order to find out what light it would throw on one or two textual problems in that great work. This manuscript is a copy in a strange hand, but it has been annotated by Beethoven himself, and anything he has written into this score is of course a priceless pointer to his mind. The Maestro examined them all carefully, and spent some time admiring others of the British Museum manuscripts.

III. Toscanini's Technique

This is a Home Service broadcast from February 1957.

When Toscanini came to London to conduct the B.B.C. Symphony Orchestra in the 1930's I think I must have listened to nearly every rehearsal. And I remember very well the first rehearsal of all. It was Brahms' Fourth Symphony, and to everyone's surprise Toscanini played the two middle movements straight through without stopping. And then he just said 'bene, bene', and referred to the score for two or three things that hadn't gone quite right, did them again, and that was all — he went on to the finale. All the same, in that very first read-through there had been many slight and subtle differences, particularly in the slow movement, though Toscanini didn't *say* anything about what he wanted, and his beat was never particularly clear. I remember I asked one of the violinists afterwards why they'd played it differently from usual, and she said she wasn't sure but she thought it was because he was generating such a high degree of concentration that they all felt it as he felt it.

Only the other day a very great English composer said to me that in his opinion some of the worst stick technique he'd ever seen on the rostrum belonged to the two greatest conductors of his time, Richter and Toscanini. This may be an exaggeration, but there's a grain of truth in it. Toscanini's beat was loose and often far from precise. I believe he got his effects in spite of it rather than because of it. Probably it was some form of hypnosis. Everyone used to say that Nikisch hypnotised his players, and certainly in the *Tristan* Prelude you could tell it was Nikisch conducting the moment the 'cellos were up on their high F in the very first bar. And Toscanini too had this really stupendous power of concentration which communicated itself to the players and made them see the music as he saw it.

Toscanini came to London with the reputation of being a very rigorous rehearser, but in fact he often finished at twelve (or soon after) a rehearsal scheduled to go on until one o'clock; and sometimes he cut rehearsals altogether. He used to say, 'If a passage has once been right, I never want to do it again'. But some of us felt that this more easy-going attitude towards our orchestras only developed as he gained experience of them. Apparently in New York he always insisted on his players giving 100 per cent of power, excitement and energy in every rehearsal. In America perhaps this is necessary. But Anglo-Saxon orchestras aren't the same. They can't work themselves up to Toscanini's pitch of tension in a morning's rehearsal, and then repeat the process in performance the same evening. And I think Toscanini came to sense that, and he was soon demanding a little less at rehearsal and getting what he wanted at the show. After all, a rehearsal is not a concert but a preparation.

He did, of course, rehearse intensively when he couldn't get what he wanted. Though his powers of concentration got him a long way, they could not get him the whole way, and his occasional fits of temper were usually due to his inability to express in English what he wanted to say; in fact, they arose out of dissatisfaction with himself. In my experience, he only once lost his temper with a player: he sensed that one of the orchestra was defying him and not doing his best, and suddenly he rushed out of the hall and the rehearsal broke up. I heard him sobbing in the artists' room. Another time he broke the back of a Brahms symphony score and threw it in two halves over his head because he couldn't find the place; it was a Breitkopf score, and he was used to the Simrock one with everything coming at a different point on the page. At the time I knew him, he was so blind that he had to hold a score right up close to his eyes in order to see the notes at all. So most of the time in rehearsal and all the time in performance he had to rely on his miraculously photographic memory.

As an illustration of this, let me offer the following story. Toscanini was staying with a friend of mine, and said he must get down to his scores for the next concert. The man offered to fetch the scores, but of course they weren't there. Toscanini hadn't brought them with him: every detail of the score was in his head. But he sat back in a chair with his eyes shut and was obviously concentrating very deeply, preparing, I suppose, the sound of the work from his memory of the printed page. Suddenly there was a growl and he seized some music paper which he had handy, and wrote down, in perfectly accurate full score, three or four bars of the Beethoven overture or whatever it was he was at work on. Having written it out, he tore it up and put it in the wastepaper basket.

Now I can only think that the point of doing that was that as he went through the work, reconstructing his ideal in his head, he suddenly came to a point at which this ideal did not come instantly to call. I wouldn't think it was as serious as a hiatus in his memory. It was probably just that the complete picture of the music did not come to him as it should. The process of writing it all out had made it more vivid in his mind and he was then able to commend it instantly.

Another instance of his extreme power of, so to speak, visualising the sound of music from the sight of the printed page was told me by an American colleague of his, who at a rehearsal heard him stop at a certain chord when he was rehearsing a brand new work by a young Italian composer for its first performance. Toscanini stopped, and said, 'where is the oboe?' The point was that the oboe should have had a note contributing to the chord, which was already doubled in another part of the orchestra. But Toscanini missed the oboe tone from the sound of that chord, even though the particular note concerned was being contributed by someone else as well. Toscanini's visual preparation of the score was so intense that the sound was also complete in his mind. I myself have heard him correct a player who began a long *diminuendo* one note before it was marked.

Before any public performance he was always in a terribly nervous state. He couldn't listen to anything you said to him, and his wife must have put up with innumerable tantrums on these occasions. She was always on hand in the artists' room, helping him to dress, and in the interval he always changed all his clothes and she had to help him then, too. I remember once he was to conduct the Beethoven Mass in D in the Queen's Hall, and he was in his usual nervous state beforehand, and three minutes before the concert was due to begin, he came up to me and said, 'Please will you tell the audience I conduct it not tonight; I conduct it next Thursday'. In horror, I tried to talk about other things, the weather, anything, and then the platform attendant appeared and said, 'Ready please, maestro', and so got him on to the platform, and all was well. Over and over again music must have caused him agonies of suffering. Once he heard some members of his New York orchestra giving a concert of string quartets, and because they were out of tune he cried all night. He had nothing else to think of but music. I never heard him talk of anything else. Bruno Walter will discuss the latest play or novel, but not Toscanini.

His tempi were sometimes on the fast side, and I don't suppose I am the only conductor who has changed his mind about the tempo of the trio in Beethoven's Seventh because of Toscanini. People used to take it much slower than they do now, but after hearing Toscanini's version I came to the conclusion we'd all been too slow, and he was quite right to take it faster. I remember his Beethoven Symphonies as great architectural elevations, west fronts, frozen music in reverse if you like, and I do not think any conductor alive today can give them the architectural quality that I associate with Toscanini.

NIKISCH

I. Nikisch Remembered

This talk was given on the B.B.C.'s Third Programme in
March 1950.

I never had a lesson from Nikisch in my life, but I learnt more
from him about conducting than from anyone else. His power
over the orchestra was quite phenomenal, and he had an
unfailing tact and understanding of the psychology of everything to do with rehearsal. With all that, he could not be
called a musician of wide sympathies. Everything was strongly coloured with his own personality, and when that exactly
fitted the work in hand, well, that was wonderful. But when it
didn't, one had to put up with a view of the masterpiece
through spectacles that were highly tinted with that amazing
gipsy colour that was never far away when Nikisch was on the
platform. Even in my days of extreme youthful enthusiasm, I
used to admit that if I had to make a list of the music I would
prefer to hear conducted by Nikisch rather than any other
conductor, that list would be small. It would include all the
Schumann and Liszt symphonies; the three Weber overtures;
a good deal of Wagner — notably *Tristan*; and the Verdi
Requiem, in which he played under Verdi's direction in Vienna
as a boy. But if it was Beethoven, well, Richter, Weingartner,
and Steinbach all seemed to do greater justice to the music;
Tchaikovsky — Safonov gave it a stronger outlook and greater
power; Brahms — Steinbach really understood it; and so on.

Several years before I went to Leipzig, I had the honour
of an introduction to Nikisch and he told me then he was soon
going to give up his conducting class at the Conservatoire, but
that he would give me a pass for all his rehearsals. He also
accepted me as a bass in the big Choral Society at the
Gewandhaus which had no chorus-master, Nikisch himself
taking every rehearsal. We sang, I think, in three concerts and
took part in the performance of the Ninth Symphony which
always closed the Gewandhaus season.

What were the special qualities in his conducting which
made, for instance, Tchaikovsky write so enthusiastically of it?

I think his greatest quality was his fabulous power over the orchestra. That long stick, held in a tiny white hand, seemed to say so much, and express so completely the music as felt by Nikisch, that a great deal of verbal explanation at rehearsal was unnecessary, and so the tension and friction of many rehearsals were avoided; and even his own wonderful left hand had less to do than most, because the stick said so much.

I often wondered whether the beauty of his gesture helped to produce the peculiar beauty of tone which came from even a second-rate orchestra when he stood before it. Certain it was that his power of finding always a *melos* (as Wagner called it), something that had to sing somewhere in the orchestra all the time, coupled with his tremendous temperament, where one often felt his Hungarian blood taking command, gave his performance a most rare beauty which could thrill us even at the same moment when we were perhaps conscious that a *rubato* was extravagant, a piece of phrasing not really in keeping with the style of the work, or a movement too fast or too slow. Perhaps this isn't a thing that can be learnt or copied, but it was the great characteristic of his conducting.

II. Nikisch and Method in Rehearsal

Sir Adrian never made any secret of the debt his own technique owed to watching Nikisch. This article is reprinted from *The Music Review*, Vol. XI, No. 2, May 1950.

Arthur Nikisch died in 1922, and his last appearance in London was in 1914. He has therefore become a legend — though I am glad to say that there are many distinguished members of London orchestras who remember him well — but he will I suppose soon be forgotten. Before this happens I feel I must put on record an impression, based on six months' close watching, of his method, particularly in the rehearsal room, for its economy and effectiveness have no equal in my experience, and should not be lost.

To begin with, he made his stick say more than any other conductor that I have ever seen. Its power of expression was so intense that one felt it would be quite impossible, for instance, to play *staccato* when Nikisch was showing a *legato*. There was no need for him to stop and ask for a *sostenuto* — his stick had already pulled it from the players, and so on, with almost every kind of nuance. It followed, then, that a most sensitive left hand could be used (albeit most sparingly and economically) to supplement the expression shown by the stick, and so there seemed that very little was left for verbal explanation.

Now when verbal explanation was necessary, Nikisch would rarely pull the orchestra up, then and there. He would play on probably to the end of a movement, by which time there might be several passages to be discussed — these could be dealt with together and the passages replayed if necessary, though he would often trust his players to remember a point once he had spoken of it, and saw no need to insist on hearing it again. Toscanini, in shorter movements, often used the same method on his London visits, playing the movement right through, and then taking up any points that needed rehearsal.

I am convinced that this method enormously saves strain to the whole orchestra — surely these rehearsal stoppages are like jamming brakes on suddenly and jerking a fine car to a standstill — and also, if the work is not well known, enables the players to get a first impression in one whole, instead of having it continually broken up. The conductor may have to keep half a dozen points in his head at once, and remember the references quickly when the times comes, but what is that to the housewife whose shopping list is in her head? I feel, too, in this connection, that with a new work, first impressions are of great importance. Now if this first impression is a string of short bursts punctuated by long dissertations on tonal balance, technique, colour, or anything else, the result in the mind of the player will hardly contribute to the long view and continuous sweep of a fine performance. The architecture of a work is of fundamental importance — so fundamental that it should be made clear to everyone at the outset, and left so firmly in the mind of the player that he conveys it of necessity — even if unconsciously — to the audience. This becomes an impossibility if every bar has to be closely examined before anyone knows how the work is going to end.

There may sometimes be points of style that are better settled at the outset; the opening figure of the *Allegro* of the Schubert Great C major, for instance, is worth stopping over at once, to get its bowing fixed once and for all. I remember many years ago a distinguished guest conductor spending the first eighteen minutes of a rehearsal worrying over a difficult *arpeggio* in bar 6 of a work. The section of the orchestra concerned with the *arpeggio* consisted mostly of some fairly hard-boiled old hands, whose attitude to the work, to the conductor, and to life in general was considerably soured by the experience, and a few shy girls, who were so petrified with fright that their contributions to the performance were reduced to something infinitesimal. The disastrous psychology of this was not remedied until the great man had gone home three days later.

In the Leipzig Gewandhaus Nikisch also had the Wednesday morning Public Rehearsal in which to work. There was a general impression that this was exactly like the concert; in fact, rehearsal-goers used sometimes to give themselves airs, and criticise the well-dressed evening audience as fashionable and non-musical. Nikisch evidently did not subscribe to this view, for he would rehearse quite blatantly in front of the rehearsal audience. He never stopped, but with left hand and eyes would indicate for instance that something had been far too loud, and should be corrected at the performance. The standard classic might not be touched at all — or perhaps only a few chosen passages taken. The rest, and all concertos, were tried for the first time at the Public Rehearsal, a procedure not always satisfactory to the more fussy and garrulous soloists!

In later life Nikisch had a curious aversion from studying scores. He was always ready to do new works, but said that he could not think out his interpretation from the cold print, but must have the living sound under his hand. His study methods (or lack of them) were once the target of that inveterate practical joker, Max Reger, who, just before Nikisch was going to start the first reading of a new work of his, shouted up from the hall, 'I say, Nikisch, may I suggest that you just run through the big double fugue before you play the work right through?' 'Certainly, my friend' was the reply, 'Gentlemen, we will begin with the big double fugue', as he turned over the pages to find it. Unfortunately there wasn't a fugue in the work at all — Reger, in pulling the leg of the great conductor, was also giving his own a good tug!

It was said that the first bar of *Tristan* was enough to enable anyone to recognise blindfold the warmth and beauty of tone which unmistakably showed that Nikisch was conducting — these things cannot be described, but there is no doubt that he fully understood Wagner's postulate: that there must always be at least one singing line in any music; the power to call this up also lay in that wonderful stick, and once he knew an orchestra he would rarely demand any special tension at rehearsals.

Here again it would seem that his practice is in danger of being forgotten for ever. All the great conductors of the present day seem to demand a hundred per cent intensity from players all through every rehearsal. This may be necessary with the Latin and Southern European types who form the majority of American orchestras, but I am convinced that with the more cold-blooded, matter-of-fact, British, Dutch and Scandinavian mentalities it is not necessary — indeed, it is dangerous to demand full intensity during a long rehearsal on the day of the concert, and those of us who were privileged to hear Toscanini's London rehearsals in 1939 felt that he too sensed this. No one expects a footballer or a boxer to exercise at full pressure for three hours on the day of an important match, and it seems hardly wise with orchestral musicians. Nikisch's rehearsals were always peaceful, almost uneventful; only once did I see him lose his temper, and rarely did he ask for more tone — he knew that that would come when wanted, and when called for by his stick.

I remember Toscanini saying 'I never rehearse again anything that has once gone well'. This excepted, of course, the final rehearsal, at which he always plays through the whole programme. I think it is true of all artistic matters that they can never stand still: there must always be improvement or the other thing; and where rehearsal is concerned, the moment one reaches the peak, the bogey of staleness begins to rear its head. Toscanini is a most economical rehearser. He was given a generous schedule in London, it is true, but he often stopped the rehearsal an hour early, and he actually cancelled one or two altogether. A member of the Philadelphia Orchestra told me recently that Stokowski also used to rehearse most sparingly, and the weekly scheme was usually after this pattern: Monday — straight through the programme; Tuesday — hard work on difficult spots (rarely more than two hours); Wednesday — reading new music; Thursday — straight through the programme, often with only a few comments. The concerts took place on Friday and Saturday.

Another aspect of conducting in which Nikisch's practice differed from that of most of his colleagues was when he was conducting as a guest — and here, too, his practice seems to be near that of Toscanini. It would seem that a stranger, conducting an orchestra for the first time, prepares, if possible, to extract from his players a performance which coincides in every detail with the perfect performance which his imagination conjures up. In many cases this will mean total destruction of an orchestra's basic style: the possibility of a Viennese conductor preparing a Mahler, or even a Beethoven Symphony with a Parisian orchestra might be quoted as an example. I can also remember two disastrous rehearsals when a distinguished foreigner (whose conducting days are now over) tried to make the B.B.C. Orchestra play the *Enigma* Variations 'as Sir Elgar told us he wished in 1908'. A critic afterwards said that he seemed to have succeeded in utterly destroying the B.B.C. Orchestra's fundamental ideas of the Variations, and had evidently not had enough rehearsal time to rebuild his own conception on top.

Nikisch would never do this. He would play well into the movement — perhaps right through it — before interrupting or commenting. He would then have seen and grasped one or more fundamental points of style where he probably felt the orchestra's playing to be furthest removed from what he felt was right. He would then take great pains to alter this at a few crucial spots, and might (if time was short) leave many other similar passages to be adapted by the players themselves. So, with a minimum of friction and discomfort to the players, he could achieve a large measure of success, and bring the performance much closer, at any rate, to his ideal.

Nikisch had a great sense of tact and contact with those with whom he was working, and M. Inghelbrecht tells in his recent book[1] how Nikisch used to say that the mentality of different members of the orchestra varied usually with the instruments they played, and that he could speak in a much more subtle and delicate way to a player on the oboe or a string leader, whereas he would put the point at issue considerably more forcibly if he was talking, say, to a player on a heavy brass instrument.

I hesitate to give advice to colleagues with equal experience to my own, but I think any orchestral player would agree that the main points I have described: avoidance of stoppages, and reduced intensity at rehearsals, would, if practised in greater measure, much ease the strain for each individual musician; and a greater continuity in playing, alternating with an intensive rehearsal of those passages that are found to need hard work, will enable the conductor to get results in a far shorter time, with less tension all round. He only needs to develop the capacity to keep in his head a list of the points to which he must go back. Nikisch, as far as I know, never wrote a line about his work, so I hope that these few notes may help others, particularly those who inherit some of his genius, to profit by his experience and his practice, which are still so vividly admired by all who remember him.

III. Nikisch and Musicians

First appearing in *Music and Letters*, vol. iii, April 1922, this essay has been reprinted in Carl Bamberger (ed.), *The Conductor's Art*, McGraw-Hill, New York, 1965.

Eloquent pens have mourned in many languages the loss of Arthur Nikisch. We have in the last few weeks been reminded of the marvellous power of exposing the beauty of any work he touched, of the personal charm and influence over those with whom he came in contact and of the broadness of view which

1. Désiré-Émile Inghelbrecht, *Le Chef d'Orchestre et son Équipe*, Julliard, Paris, 1949; translated as *The Conductor's World*, Nevill, London, 1953.

caused him to study and follow the music of many nations and many periods; and it is these qualities which have endeared him to audiences in many countries. But it may not be without interest to examine for a moment the side of him which some of us would venture to assert was the greatest of all — his power as a conductor in the narrowest and most technical sense of the word.

We know that technique in all things is the ability to make use of our means with the least effort and the greatest effect, and here surely Arthur Nikisch was supreme. His loss must seem to other conductors almost comparable to the loss of the dies at the Mint or the destruction of the standard measures at Greenwich; or even worse than this, for the means of reproduction or replacement are more complete in these latter cases. Consciously or unconsciously — and we are inclined to think it was instinct and the effortless outcome of long experience that brought him to this perfection — he always seemed to secure his results in the simplest way possible with the slightest movement and the greatest beauty. I can remember the most thrilling performance of the Brahms C minor Symphony that I have ever heard — we are not now discussing whether Brahms should be thrilling or not — and at the end, when the orchestra and audience had been worked up to a white heat and the movement had finished in a blaze of triumph, it occurred to me that Nikisch's hand had never been raised higher than the level of his face throughout the whole movement. The long stick held by those tiny fingers almost buried beneath an enormous shirt-cuff had been really covering quite a small circle the whole time, though the range of expression had been so wide; and surely if the arm had ever been stretched to its full length, some catastrophe must have occurred, like an earthquake or the destruction of the building.

He did not spare only his own physique, but also the strain to the forces he controlled. Two interesting examples of this may be quoted. In Amsterdam in 1920 I was present at all the rehearsals before his first concert — he had not been there for twenty-four years. He began rehearsing the D minor Symphony of Schumann. All was quiet and restful, even cold; a great deal was shown by gesture though always with the utmost restraint, and of real excitement there was none. Suddenly, where the last movement becomes 'schneller' near the end, his wrist seemed to start a dynamo and there was an unexpected dramatic intensity about the two crashes and intervening silences. The second pause in particular seemed endless, when with a whispered 'Eins, zwei', he led the basses off into their final passage, and the excitement of those last twenty-six bars of *presto* so roused the orchestra that they got up and cheered. By this time the master was quite calm again and for the rest of the three rehearsals there was no other moment of tension. He had taken the full measure of his orchestra in those few moments and there was no need for anything but quiet work until the concert. A still more remarkable instance of this was at the Leeds Festival in 1913. The interest of the chorus at the arrival of the great Nikisch was intense, and he, as usual, perfectly sure of himself, knowing every member of the orchestra and trusting the reputation of the chorus, took a risk that none but he would have taken and started the rehearsal with a work with which he had obviously the very slightest acquaintance — Richard Strauss' *Taillefer*. He went right through the work with hardly a stop and at a very deliberate pace, and I do not think he looked up from the music more than six times. He then played a few passages again and shut up the score. The chorus were obviously in despair, as he had not once given them the slightest 'lift'; and a distinguished musician who was sitting next to me said, 'Surely to goodness he is not going to leave it in that state?' He then went on to the familiar first-act selection from *Parsifal*, when he was able to get on intimate terms with the chorus, and I am told that the performance of Strauss' battle picture was as full of fire and excitement as anyone could have wished.

At home in Leipzig in his own hall with his own orchestra Nikisch had reduced everything to the lowest possible output of effort. The weekly arrangement there was a private rehearsal on Tuesday evening (to which we students were given cards of admission); the public rehearsal on Wednesday morning, which was filled with the musical people of Leipzig, who used to tell you it was 'exactly the same as the concert, only the audiences were much more intelligent'; and the fashionable subscription concert on Thursday evening, where seats and boxes were handed down from father to son and for which it was very difficult to buy a single ticket. It was an accident that took me to the second Gewandhaus concert of the season during which I was a student. I had been to the Wednesday morning rehearsal and had there been disgusted to hear the violins play the opening tune of the slow movement of the *Jupiter* Symphony in canon *divisi*, the second half playing the tune at a quaver's distance from the first half. Various other things, notably continual exaggerations of expression and an extraordinary looseness of ensemble, were all swallowed by the complacent 'musical' audience with complete equanimity. Coming to the conclusion that if Nikisch treated Leipzig audiences like this I preferred to hear him in London, I almost refused the kind offer by a friend of a ticket for the evening concert. However, I went, and was rewarded with one of the most perfect Mozart performances I have ever heard. From then on I went whenever possible to both rehearsals and the concert, and it was often amusing to note how Nikisch would finish the private rehearsal in an hour or so, perhaps not touching a big work like the Schubert Great C major; how he would then blatantly rehearse the Symphony in front of his Wednesday audience, which happily drank in the absurd *rubati* and other exaggerations; and how these things would all drop into proportion at the concert and fine performances result, even though one did not perhaps go all the way with the master in his 'readings' of Beethoven or the Slavonic — or rather Magyar — passion he infused into Brahms.

Particularly at the time when Nikisch first came to London a great deal was said about his mesmerising the orchestra, and the press contained quotations from statements of orchestral musicians to the effect that they 'felt unlike themselves' when playing under his direction. Such things are difficult to discuss and even more difficult to gauge, but it may be possible to think of certain causes contributory to this impression. One of our most distinguished orchestral players whom I happened to meet a few minutes after he had finished rehearsing recently with Dr. Strauss said to me, 'I have been playing the passages in *Don Juan* and *Till Eulenspiegel* for the first time for many years'. The meaning of this was, of course, that although Strauss' beat looked rather wooden, it was in fact most sympathetic and flexible, and he would give a little time wherever it was needed to avoid a scramble; but so little that the ordinary hearer would be unaware of any *rubato*. In things of this kind Nikisch was quite remarkable; his long experience as an orchestral player, coupled with a remarkable sympathy which also showed itself in his conducting of concertos and opera, made it easy for him to do things that would never occur to most people. Another example of this was the way he would let the length of a pause or a *ritardando* depend on the bowing of the string players. Again, his experience helped him to glance always at the right man in the orchestra, however they were grouped and however deeply they were concealed behind a voluminous music stand. The curious slow gaze with which he seemed to take in the whole orchestra at the beginning of most rehearsals and of every concert gave him an opportunity of noticing everything and at the same time of getting on to terms with everyone.

Under such conducting it is easy for players to 'feel unlike themselves' and for observers to think they are being mesmerised, but no amount of technical competence will account for the fact, agreed on by everybody, that from the first note of any performance the actual tone of the instruments seemed different from the tone produced by any other conductor. This shows a remarkable personal power, and there are few others of whom it is true. No one will forget the extraordinary way in which he compelled his audience to listen and made concentration child's play from beginning to end of a long concert or opera. This is, of course, a power common to all great artists, although the nature of the attraction varies. I can remember the impression made by Paderewski, who seemed to plunge us into the very presence of Beethoven or Chopin or whoever it might be. Nikisch rather brought us face to face with Nikisch, and it was only when his temperament matched that of the composer that the greatest performances would result. I would almost go so far as to say that there were few works that I would not have felt could have been better given by other conductors, in spite of the marvellous fascination of Nikisch's art.

But whatever he touched was alive and warm, and

vitality is the alpha and omega of executive music. In all Wagner (except perhaps *Die Meistersinger*), often in Mozart and Haydn and always in Weber, his performances were supreme, and another landmark was the Verdi *Requiem* at Leeds in 1913. Even when we felt we must disagree there was such poetry and beauty, not to mention technical mastery, that we were held spellbound; and now all musicians and music lovers can only mourn together the loss of a great personality, a lovable man and a marvellous artist.

FURTWÄNGLER

This essay is reprinted from Sir Adrian's book *Thoughts on Conducting*, published by Phoenix House, London, in 1963 and now out of print.

Furtwängler was a dedicated and intensely emotional conductor. His stick, in comparison to Nikisch's, was inexpressive and difficult to follow. Furtwangler's actual behaviour at a concert was something that made players extremely frightened, very often because they felt that body and soul might not keep together. His beat, particularly to orchestras that didn't know him well, was extremely puzzling and there were very often several at once — a sort of shaky, vibrant repetition of the beat, which made the audience wonder which of the repetitions was going to be chosen by the orchestra for the impact of the sound. It always seemed a miracle that they did in fact come in together, for we never could be certain which beat they were going to choose; Furtwängler's concentration chose for them.

Now that, extended over a concert, had, I remember, a very sharp effect on at least one distinguished player in the orchestra, who said that he was worn out at the end of the concert with the effort of finding out where he was and playing his part in the ensemble and in an ensemble that was an ensemble. And I am inclined to think that it was this tension, this uncertainty, that contributed a great deal to the magnetic power and warmth of the tone quality that came from Furtwängler's performances. If an orchestra doesn't quite know where it is, it plays with a certain intensity that contributes enormously to the vitality of the performance. The players as they play are really not sure whether they will put a foot wrong at any moment in any bar, and so they play with a certain excited vitality that contributes something remarkable to the power of the performance as a whole.

This brings us immediately to the question of a conductor who has a superbly clear beat. Then the orchestra know where they are, but they may not be on their toes to that extent and perhaps may not give so vital a performance. That is always a possibility.

It is, of course, conceivable that there are conductors who, having command of a good deal of rehearsal time, get a great deal of perfection, and use a technique so precise and easy to follow that the players sink back and need some other stimulus to make the performance vital. I can't think of any extreme case of that, but it could be a great danger that a man who is in complete command of his technique, which might be reasonably expressive, gets as a result dull performances when he's not on the top of his form, and particularly perhaps when he's thinking too much on architectural lines.

I feel sure that it is extremely useful for a conductor in this country, who has very little rehearsal time, to have that extreme clarity. He can get over to the orchestra very quickly what he wants and make it clear to them.

BEECHAM

Also from *Thoughts on Conducting*. In fact, Sir Adrian often found himself out of sympathy with Beecham's interpretations, but was always at pains not to reveal his views.

Sir Thomas Beecham's power over the orchestra was similar to Furtwangler's. A most expressive stick, movements that were out of proportion when one compared them with the wonderful economy of people like Nikisch and Bruno Walter, but a wholehearted concentration and a wonderful power of expression. In fact, very often he was able to persuade us that music that we had hitherto thought wasn't quite in the front rank was all the same something particularly lovely. It appealed so to him that he infectiously made it appeal to us.

It was almost a hypnotic appeal that he had over the orchestra. And with Beecham, too, it was perhaps even more an improvisation than it was with Furtwängler or Nikisch. It was quite well known in the orchestral world and recognised that what Beecham rehearsed he was not necessarily going to do at the performance. He might whip up something quite differently and in quite a different proportion. But it didn't matter. It was a lovely and lively experience that could be enjoyed by the whole audience as a *tour de force* and as a brilliant piece of musical exposition.

WOOD

I. Wood's Achievement

Sir Adrian wrote this assessment of his older colleague's career early in 1962.

It is not too much to say that the backbone of London orchestral music for at least forty years was centred in the person of Sir Henry J. Wood. The Queen's Hall was opened in 1893 and the Promenade Concerts began two years later. Although for a few seasons the programmes could be described only as lightweight, by the turn of the century the main classics had all taken a permanent place there, and important novelties were added to the repertory each year. As well as the Proms, Sir Henry was responsible for twenty-six Sunday afternoon concerts each winter, and these also covered the whole range of classical music and samples of the modern, and only twelve Saturday afternoons for many years international artists contributed music with which they were specially associated.

At the age of twelve in 1901, I was sent to Westminster School and given a season ticket to the Symphony and Sunday concerts. Admission to the balcony on Sundays was 1/6d, but a transferable season ticket for the twenty-six concerts cost, I think, two guineas.

For six or seven years I never missed a concert, and my notes in the scores show that most Beethoven Symphonies, and a great deal of what is still the current repertoire, recurred continually — many of them every year. And at the Symphony Concerts the fare was enriched by the appearance of Debussy to conduct the *Nocturnes* and *L'Après-midi d'un Faune*, or Strauss with the first English performance of *Ein Heldenleben*, with artists of the calibre of Kreisler, Ysaÿe and Busoni. I can specially remember the astonishment caused by Raoul Pugno, who played Mozart concertos, which were then unknown in London.

There is no doubt that Sir Henry was one of the greatest masters of the craft of conducting. For many years the Proms had only three rehearsals for the six concerts each week, and in order that the programme should be adequately rehearsed, every detail was thought out beforehand, and not only the scores, but every orchestral part, was marked by him, even to the point of showing where the beat would be split in a *rallentando*, so there could be no mistake whether there had been time to rehearse the passage or not. Later he was given one rehearsal for each concert, but he never knew the present luxury of two rehearsals for each concert and two orchestras in each week.

His use of the stick, too, was masterly. It was unusually long and provided with a large cork handle, which enabled him to get a balanced swing by holding this stick at the end close to the handle at the point of balance, so that the fingers could direct the movement with practically no effort, as the stick and handle balanced each other. He was thus able to conduct three three-hour rehearsals with a minimum of fatigue. The stick he used at his last concert, together with the score of Beethoven's Seventh Symphony, are to be seen in a room devoted to his memory, close to the entrance door of the

Royal Academy of Music. Students who visit this room may be surprised to see how thoroughly he marked the score of this well-worn Symphony. He did not claim that it was a good thing to mark scores in this way — in fact I can remember his speaking in rather a disparaging way of the practice — but I am quite sure that I should do the same if I ever had to face the ordeal of eight or ten weeks of nightly concerts. The risk of a momentary loss of concentration would be considerable, and a gentle reminder amply justified.

It has been a constant source of surprise through my life, when some newish work has made a stir at a London concert, to find that Sir Henry had probably given two or three performances of it a year or two before. These works, too, have only come to his programmes after careful examination and thought, and the list of 'young British' works which he examined before accepting them must be enormous. I noticed an interesting practice connected with these examinations. On pages 9, 19, 29, 39 and so on of a manuscript score, one could see in the blackest part of the page, where notes were thickest, an unobtrusive 'H.J.W.' pencilled into the score. I can only imagine that some composers, annoyed at the rejection of their work, would put a new cover on it and send it in again under an assumed name. Sir Henry was not easily bamboozled!

He told me another delightful story of his handling of a difficult moment in the history of the Queen's Hall Orchestra. The contract for this was not a full-time one, but included eight or ten weeks of Promenades, the twenty-six Sunday afternoons (at reduced fees as there was no rehearsal), the Symphony Concerts on many a Saturday afternoon, together with any other dates in and out of London which had been collected before the contract was issued. A year or two before the 1914 War, when the Orchestra was being backed by a wealthy syndicate, Sir Henry was given an extra weekly repertoire rehearsal on Friday morning through the season. He was to use it for Saturdays, Sundays, or anything else that he wished, but a few days before he was starting for a holiday abroad, he heard that a few people were trying to add a stipulation that these Fridays should cover only the Sunday programme, and a further rehearsal would be demanded for anything else. As time was short he sent telegrams to the whole Orchestra inviting their attendance at Queen's Hall at 9 a.m. on the day he was leaving for abroad. He just said this: 'Good morning, ladies and gentlemen, I am sorry to have called you together so early, but I felt I must speak to you before I go for my holiday at 11 o'clock this morning. I hear, ladies and gentlemen, that there is a move afoot to restrict our new Friday rehearsal to music for the following Sunday concert. I had not expected this, but I can of course cheerfully agree to this restriction if you wish. I would just remind you that it will not be very amusing for any of us if we start rehearsing the *Tannhäuser* Overture desk by desk. Good morning, ladies and gentlemen.' He heard no more of the proposed stipulation!

There are naturally many stories of this superb craftsman still going round the orchestral world, but there are none which do not carry an undercurrent of the affection in which he was held by all the musicians he worked with, by the enormous public which has flocked to the Proms through more than fifty years, and by the winter audiences which can remember so many fine performances, carried on without interruption through two wars and the happier years between.

II. Wood the Man

This short talk was broadcast on the B.B.C.'s Home Service in 1954.

Although I can't claim to remember the first season of the Proms, I think I must have been there by 1902. So I can certainly remember fifty years of them, and in those early days, when I was still a schoolboy, there were of course all sorts of operatic fantasies and ballads in the programme which you just don't get at all nowadays — the musical side wasn't taken so seriously then. In those days, too, they used to have a demonstration of moving pictures upstairs in the small Queen's Hall during the twenty-minute interval — and very crude and shaky they were.

From the age of thirteen to nineteen I hardly missed one

of Sir Henry Wood's Sunday and Symphony concerts. I spent all my pocket money on miniature scores which in those days were astonishingly cheap, and it was Wood who introduced me to practically all the classical symphonies and concertos. I used particularly to worship his Tchaikovsky and Wagner in those days, though later I found some of his readings a little too *rubato* for my taste (although actually this turning away from *rubato* is probably not so much a matter of *my* taste but rather that of musicians generally in recent years). When I was young there seemed nothing wrong with this style of playing at all. And, of course, Wood's stick technique and rehearsal methods were always an object-lesson for any young conductor, and I feel I owe him a tremendous debt for all he taught me.

It was only after I joined the B.B.C. that I had the very real pleasure of getting to know Wood the man. I remember one hilarious afternoon at his house at Chorley Wood playing tennis with him and his two daughters, the worst game of tennis that even I ever played, for Wood was, to say the least of it, not talented in this direction, and I was even worse. Even worse, indeed, than Vaughan Williams, who used to maintain that his tennis was 'all miss and giggle'.

III. Wood's Working Methods

This section is reprinted from *Thoughts on Conducting*.

The fundamental difference between Wood and Thomas Beecham, was that Beecham would improvise at a performance, and bring off that performance; with Wood it was all carefully and accurately prepared.

Everything was in his mind; the scores were all marked, the parts were all marked and the whole thing went through (mainly because of lack of rehearsal time) according to plan.

His rehearsal technique was as completely successful and well-thought-out as everything else concerned with his art. He planned his rehearsals to the minute, in fact, to the half-minute. And soloists and concertos and everything all fell into that scheme exactly. He would very often play straight through a work at rehearsal, as he had a strong feeling that mistakes might occur in anything that had not been played, actually played on the morning of a performance. And so he would do what a good many of us would think would perhaps incline the orchestra to dullness, by playing straight through a work, not really minding how well it was being played. He might shout a comment, that such and such a passsage should be louder or softer, but he wouldn't necessarily stop and do it again.

During the Promenade season when he was working very hard, he would save his arm a certain amount by letting his leader conduct. In this case he would go into the circle of Queen's Hall and sit with a little dinner bell which he would ring if he wanted to stop and comment on anything. It was on record that this dinner bell sometimes disappeared mysteriously, but another one always appeared the next day. I think there was a store of them concealed somewhere.

Wood excelled in giving a clear performance of a work and putting it over so faithfully that one could go away and think it out for oneself afterwards and not have another mind in between one and the work, as one might have with Furtwängler or Beecham. There is no doubt that his ideal, as regards the mood and the musicianship of a performance, was always to produce a faithful reproduction of the composer's will, with no varnishing and no embellishments from the performer. He was the kind of performer who prefers to feel that he is the servant of the composer without adding something to the composition or interposing his own personality between the composer and the audience.

That was why composers of his day were delighted when he would give a first performance of a work because they knew that it would come over absolutely crystal clear and if anybody afterwards liked to start an individual interpretation of it, well, that would be all right, but first of all Wood put the thing before the public clearly as the composer had written it. I think his ideal was to present a National Gallery of musical art, but not an Exhibition Extraordinary — to be thought-provoking in a different way.

IV. Wood Remembered

On the evening of Sir Henry's death (19 August 1944) Sir
Adrian broadcast this tribute in the B.B.C.'s Home News
Bulletin.

On Friday, 28th July — less than a month ago — Sir Henry
Wood, besides conducting an aria for Miss Joan Hammond
and a concerto for Mr. Maurice Cole, gave us a performance
of Beethoven's Seventh Symphony which will not easily be
forgotten by anyone who heard it. It swept us along with all
the torrential energy of that immortal work, and any stranger
who was listening at home might well have thought that the
performance was in the charge of some brilliant young
conductor in his early forties. Those of us who were privileged
to be there were thrilled once again by our old friend's
perennial energy and perennial youth, and could never have
believed that this was his own last homage to Beethoven.

In this Jubilee year, when so many tributes have poured
in from all over the civilised world, it has been a moving
experience for many of us to read all that has been said of
Henry Wood by his friends and colleagues everywhere. Two
of his many qualities stand out again and again: his amazing
breadth of sympathy for every progressive school and every
honest composer, and his selfless service to all music, including, as it did, his unassuming readiness to allow composer or
soloist to take all the laurels at a public performance.

Indefatigable worker as he was, he must surely have been
well content to ring the curtain down on that notable broadcast last month; though all his friends, and, as I very well
know, those in the orchestra, were longing to see him back for
the actual fiftieth birthday of the Proms on 10th August.

That was not to be; so we must let our own memories
take us back to countless hours of musical initiation and
familiar delight in the Queen's Hall. We look forward to the
new Sir Henry Wood Hall; in fact, we must see that our
subscriptions make it a worthy memorial, and thus show our
gratitude that the English musical world has been so immensely blessed by the work and life of Henry Wood.

WALTER

I. Walter the Architect

This tribute was made by Sir Adrian at the beginning of the
Anglo-Austrian Music Society's Concert in the Royal Festival
Hall in February 1962.

You will know that this Concert is being given by the
Anglo-Austrian Music Society, of which Bruno Walter was a
much respected Honorary President, and so we feel that we
should like to ask you to think a little of the debt we owe this
great man.

He first came to London over fifty years ago, and in spite
of the wars, has been a constant visitor since. Many of us will
remember his splendid opera performances at Covent
Garden — Wagner, Mozart, Strauss. And I can well remember how eagerly my colleagues in the B.B.C. Symphony
Orchestra all looked forward to his visits to us.

We mourn his loss, and we feel all sympathy with his
daughter, who lived with him. But we still have many
wonderful recordings, and there is another thing. I find as I
look back on many great performances I have heard, that the
recollection of them is something more than a passing impression of beautiful sound. It has been well said that
architecture is frozen music. Surely the music can be said to
be molten architecture. And so for me, a great performance
stays with me almost as something architectural, and I look
back on the work and its performance with feelings akin to
those when one stands before a great cathedral and drinks in
its beauty.

So I would suggest, while we mourn the loss of a great
man, whose own great sorrows in life matured and glorified
his own splendid performances, we can borrow from the
Society of Friends the attitude of thankfulness to God for the
splendid life and work of Bruno Walter.

II. Walter's Technique

This is another essay from *Thoughts on Conducting* of 1963.

Furtwängler succeeded Nikisch both in Berlin and Leipzig after his death in 1922, but I cannot help feeling that the greatest opera conductor and the greatest concert conductor in the twenty and thirty years after Nikisch's death was Bruno Walter. He had, of course, a wonderful training with Mahler in Vienna, and when in 1912 he took over in Munich he was ready to give the most superb performances of operas of many differing fields.

I was lucky enough to hear his first performance in Munich in 1912 of the three great Mozart operas. Then, during the war he did a very great deal, even with all the difficulties of wartime work, to encourage and display the work of German composers. People like Walter Braunfels and Hans Pfitzner owed everything to Bruno Walter at that time. And when one was able to get back to Munich in the 'twenties, Walter was in command of a wonderful ensemble, in command of every school of opera, with the option of using three different houses, each ideally suited to the style of opera that was being performed.

His stick technique was simple and economical and there was no question that he was giving himself completely to any work that he took over. I have seen him white as a sheet after a symphonic performance; a work like the Schubert C major would tax him to the utmost. But that was the nature of his concentration and the nature of his outlook on music. And music as a mission, something that could inspire and make finer people, not only of those taking part, but of those listening in the audience, was the ideal of this great man.

That sense of dedication was a great force, almost a moral force, one might say. It is rare among performers, perhaps, but I have met it not only in Walter. There are others. They belong to the type of artist who never seems to place himself between the music and the people to whom he is playing or before whom he is conducting. Yehudi Menuhin is one. I feel with him, as I felt with Walter, that the music always comes first and was of first consequence all the time.

Walter was and Menuhin is very much the same in their
outlook on music — and one should add Casals too. I know, in
the work that they have done together, all those three, that
they have been the greatest friends.

Then there was Walter's contact with the orchestra; it
was as magnetic as that of any conductor I have mentioned. It
was got by rather different means from Toscanini and certainly different from Furtwängler. It was the man's complete
sincerity that came from him to the players and so to the
audience, that and his unfailing humanity. His idea was that
every member of his orchestra was a human being who
thought and breathed and loved his music just as he did
himself, and was always to be encouraged to do so more and
more.

In his rehearsals he stopped a fair amount. He had very
clear ideas about what he wanted and he perhaps went into
detail more than most conductors. He could make active use
of a long period of rehearsal in such a way that the orchestra
was fascinated and wanted to go further. I expect many of our
readers will have heard the two delightful records that have
been published of a rehearsal with Bruno Walter of a Mozart
symphony and I can cordially recommend it as a tonic to see
how a great man can dedicate himself to the spiritual importance of music, even while he is dealing with technical points,
in a record.

COMPOSERS AS CONDUCTORS

The following three essays are reprinted from
Thoughts on Conducting.

I. Richard Strauss

Richard Strauss was a conductor who, although he might be
expected when conducting the works of other composers, to
interpose his own very strong personality, did not do so. He
was a model of economy; in fact, I would put only him, and

Weingartner, beside Nikisch. He was one of the most economical conductors I have experienced in my life.

Like Henry Wood, he was very professional. He was an
easy rehearser, but a very intense rehearser of things that
mattered to him. I remember that the rather ominous summer
of 1914 was lit up by a wonderful performance that Richard
Strauss gave of his three early tone poems, followed by the
Mozart G minor, K.550. It is said that being given six hours
rehearsal, he disposed of his own work in less than an hour
and spent the remaining five working on the G minor. It
certainly was a wonderful performance and obviously the
result of much thought and preparation and precision of
rehearsal.

In particular the surprising slow tempi of the first and
last movements struck us at that time, and the fact that it did
not seem at all slow, simply because he was spacing his
accentuation, particularly in the bass instruments, so cleverly
and so widely that two bars seemed like one in accentuation
and therefore the music seemed to flow along quite fast,
although it was (to anyone who thought about it), going
considerably slower than the performances we were in the
habit of hearing. A thoughtful friend of mine has linked
Strauss' precise rehearsal craftsmanship with his love of card
games; his care in planning his resources in rehearsal was
parallel with his playing of a hand of his favourite skat.

II. Elgar

I suppose we use composers as conductors more in this
country than in other countries. Elgar, of course, conducted
his own works with great authority. I have been asked often if
he was a good conductor. He was and he wasn't. Nobody I
have ever met will admit that they have ever heard a finer
performance of an Elgar work than those conducted by Elgar
himself. And there is no question about it, he had a particular
sense of that nervous power that did make his music. Now it
doesn't always apply that a composer is a really fine conductor of his own music. Many of them are efficient conductors
and get quite good results, except that they get too excited to

start with and the whole thing lacks balance and structure and
a sense of climax. Strauss, of course, was such an experienced
conductor that he could do it all right. But then Strauss did
conduct other people's music as well as his own; Elgar did so
only for a short period in middle life, when he was engaged to
conduct a tour and a whole season by the London Symphony
Orchestra. It was not a great success, and didn't last very
long. It was chiefly as a conductor of his own music that he is
remembered.

(Another weakness shown by most composer-conductors
comes from their inability to hear what is happening because
rather than conducting they hear what they want to hear, and
fail to get a balanced performance because their ears are so
full of what they know is there. If it isn't there, they don't
notice it. They have their vision of the work as they originally
heard it and wrote it down and they can't really find out how
what they are actually hearing differs from their vision and
put into words the difference, so that the players concerned,
and singers, can adapt themselves to it. They cannot get
outside their own music.)

III. Vaughan Williams

Vaughan Williams always gave a most memorable performance of the *London* Symphony — it is sad that this was never
recorded. Many passages where most of us are tempted to
linger a bit, and make the most of the expressiveness, were
simply played through by him: he didn't want any nonsense
about it, and it could carry its own message without embel-
lishment. He rushed through it and somehow it sounded
absolutely splendid. I'm afraid I should never dare to copy his
reading.

There was a good story about a particularly fine performance which he conducted in Buffalo, U.S.A. He always
marked his own scores a good deal to help him to conduct, in
very large blue pencil; and particularly where there were bars
moving fast — one in a bar or two in a bar — he numbered the
bars so that he could feel his way along as he went. The score
which he had marked for this Buffalo performance suddenly

disappeared just before the performance took place, and he had to use another virgin copy, which made him very angry, with the result that the performance gained magnificently in intensity. He was rather amused to tell the story afterwards, because the full score was discovered very close to him. It had been shut up inside the grand piano!

When Vaughan Williams took over the London Bach Choir, he asked the Committee to allow him to have no concert at all for the whole of the first winter, but to devote it to the study of Bach's *St. Matthew Passion*. At the end, when Easter time came, he gave about half a dozen performances of it, in various places, with different sections of the choir. It was a most moving and interesting performance. I heard the first of them. He took some arbitrary liberties with Bach which are not perhaps to everyone's taste, and these he developed more and more as he developed to the annual performances which made such a deep impression in connection with the Dorking Festivals, and were repeated with the Hallé Orchestra in Manchester, a year or two before his death.

The paramount impression on me, when I first heard the London *St. Matthew Passion*, before Vaughan Williams had done it very many times, was that it was not a fine piece of conducting in that sense at all. It was that a very great musician indeed had worked for six months with a large number of intelligent people, and at the end of it he had impressed the whole choir with his own view of the Bach *St. Matthew Passion* so that the production of it was not at all a piece of conducting. The performance could not proceed except as it had been rehearsed and rehearsed: Bach through the spectacles of Ralph Vaughan Williams. The performance of the *St. Matthew Passion* was a spiritual matter with Vaughan Williams.

SOLOISTS AS CONDUCTORS

This is the final essay to be reproduced from Thoughts on
Conducting.

Bruno Walter sometimes liked to play and conduct a concerto
at the same time. In the small Mozarteum at Salzburg with a
group of the Vienna Philharmonic sitting round him, there
were enchanting performances of Mozart piano concertos.

In my B.B.C. days we tried to transport that to Queen's
Hall. There, of course, it seemed necessary to have a rather
bigger orchestra, and the intimacy disappeared altogether. To
anyone who had heard the Salzburg performances, the
Queen's Hall performance was quite a disappointment. And I
think that brings us back to the ordinary tradition of music-
making. If a piano plays with a certain number of string
players, more than a quintet is not usually very satisfactory. It
is true that Walter had a good many more than a quintet at
Salzburg, but there is a limit to the number that you can have.

In America where this concerto playing and conducting
had become rather a feature, for a year or two about ten years
ago, I heard José Iturbi playing the Grieg, with the Philadelphia Orchestra, and that ought to have been all right in
all conscience. But it most emphatically was not. The famous
scales in the last movement finish with a crack of the full
orchestra (which I admit are rather a terror to the conductor — I'm never quite happy about them myself), but on this
occasion Iturbi got comfortably to the A at the top of the scale
and the orchestra came in comfortably on its crash an
appreciable split second after he had finished his scale.

I know that Mitropoulos has sometimes played even
Prokofiev concertos with the New York orchestra, but I
cannot feel that it is ever really satisfactory. Control from the
keyboard is just not practical politics with an orchestra larger
than twenty or twenty-five. It may have been all very well in
Bach's day, though there are many of us who are not quite
sure that the performances that Bach heard of his own works
were quite as perfect as they should be nowadays.

That brings us to the solo player who likes to conduct
without necessarily giving up his instrument. Certain artists

who are great teachers have also been conductors of considerable character.

First of all in this connection I think of Pablo Casals. I
had the great experience of spending a month in Barcelona in
the days when he spent a very great deal of time and money
conducting an orchestra which he collected there. It was a
delightfully easy-going Spanish kind of procedure. I remember the rehearsals finished each evening at 12.30 a.m. He
rehearsed very thoroughly, as one would chamber music, and
I had the pleasure of listening to the detailed rehearsals of
many varied things. Casals' range of interest was surprising,
spreading naturally over the great Viennese period, but
including Stravinsky, Saint-Saëns, and many other composers
of all schools. He was a great teacher and for that reason,
when he came to London after the formation of the B.B.C.
Symphony Orchestra, we often asked him to conduct a
Sunday afternoon concert, at the same time that he played the
'cello at one of the Wednesday evening Queen's Hall concerts.
We always learnt a very great deal and in particular I can
remember very fine performances of the Brahms *Tragic* Overture and the Schubert C major Symphony conducted by him.

In more recent times Mr. Menuhin has taken to conducting string organisations. He usually leads as well and I always
think that when a small string combination plays with a
leader of that calibre, provided the bass is also led by a
musician of some sensitiveness and understanding, a performance of a peculiar lilt and beauty can emerge, such as can very
often elude even the most sensitive stick.

Going back to Casals, I think it was with him a pretty
stern rule that he would never play the 'cello on occasions
when he was conducting. He certainly never conducted a
'cello concerto which he was himself playing and always kept
the two functions entirely separate. His rehearsal technique
seemed more like a lesson from a great teacher than anything
else. And his stick technique also contributed to that, in that
he did not trouble very much to make his stick an expressive
instrument.

But when he was rehearsing, he would teach them
actually how to play their instruments, bowing and phrasing,
as well as interpretation. He was very much interested in the

technique of the various instrumentalists, particularly, of course, in the stringed instruments. But also he would use that method with the wind as well.

PART THREE

ON CONDUCTING

THE CONDUCTOR'S JOB

Sir Adrian contributed this talk to a series, 'Professional Musician', broadcast on the B.B.C.'s Forces Network in February 1947.

When I was a boy I was brought up to think that anyone who talked about his own job was a profound bore. But as I've grown older, I've had so many people asking questions, and even inviting me to give a talk on my job, that I have given up apologising, as it certainly seems to be something of a mystery to those who only see a conductor at his concert.

In musical and general education the conductor must be unusually well equipped. He must have a great deal of general musical knowledge; and I don't mean just of orchestral scores. He must also have a working knowledge of all the instruments with which he is to come in contact, including the human voice. Many years ago I was lucky enough to have a lesson twice a week for a long time with a bandmaster. He brought one wind instrument with him to each lesson, and we worked away at the trombone, or the clarinet, or whatever it was, often for several weeks. I could take it home in between until I could understand the fingering, and then we went on to another instrument. I had lessons in violin, viola and singing at other times.

A good many conductors started life as orchestral players. For instance, Toscanini and Barbirolli were 'cellists, and Koussevitzky a great double-bass player. You can learn a lot about conducting by playing in the orchestra; for instance,

you discover the sort of stick-work from the conductor that
helps the player to get a good ensemble, and also the sort of
gesture that puts them off and makes the playing ragged. I
would add that I personally am often glad that in my teens I
tried my hand at composition, for I feel that the composer's
mind cannot be too closely understood by one who would
interpret.

So much for the preliminaries. Now let us follow our
conductor into his study where there are three or four new
scores which he has to prepare for performance in a few weeks'
time. Remember, these scores have in them every note that is
played by every instrument, so they take a bit of looking at.
How is the conductor to get a knowledge of those scores so
that he can, before the first rehearsal, form a clear picture of
his interpretation? He's got to decide how fast, and how loud
every single instrument is to play, exactly how each passage is
to be phrased, and above all, how the work is to build up to
and from its climaxes, in order that he may present it to the
audience as a single whole, inevitably moving forward from its
first note to its last. Personally, I always believe in trying to
get a clear picture in my head of the work as a whole — as an
art critic might walk backwards to a point from which he can
see a large picture in one glance, before he examines the detail
of each part of it. So I try and get my bird's-eye view by
silently reading through the work at a very fast pace, much
faster than it can be played. After I've done this several times
I begin to see the whole work in perspective, and then I can
get slowly down to details page by page, and so gradually
become familiar with the work and clear in my mind as to how
it should be made to sound.

As I develop my own work, and watch my colleagues
also, I become more and more convinced of the importance of
method in rehearsal. The psychology of the handling of a
hundred high-spirited artists is no easy matter, and a boring
rehearsal is not likely to result in a brilliant concert. Some
conductors stop at every little thing that goes wrong, and the
unfortunate orchestra sometimes goes right through a three-
hour rehearsal without everyone playing more than ten bars
consecutively. The result is they never get any idea of the
music as a whole at all. I believe in playing any unfamiliar

piece straight through if possible without stopping, and then going back to tackle the difficulties. And if it is a new work with manuscript parts I always pray that the parts are fairly accurately copied. A few wrong notes are inevitable and of course it's the conductor's job to spot them and put them right — no easy matter in a *very* modern work. But if the parts are full of mistakes, the conductor may have to spend all his rehearsal in getting them right and then there's no time left for the real business of rehearsal at all.

But with well-known music a competent orchestra will take a very great deal 'as read' if properly handled, and there is a great deal that can be left without comment. For instance, in a classical symphony, once the style is established there are long passages which can only be played in one way, and present no technical difficulty, and these can even be skipped altogether if rehearsal time is short, as it usually is.

Orchestras vary a great deal in different countries — in some they expect the conductor to go through a difficult passage in detail, quite slowly perhaps, discussing fingering, and bowing, and so on; whereas in others the players accept responsibility themselves for providing the right notes in the right way, and it is up to the conductor to start from that point and go on with the rehearsal of his ideas of interpretation.

Wind instruments find it much harder than strings to play together because of the time-lag in horns and heavy brass, between the moment the player blows and the moment the sound comes out the other end. The *Midsummer Night's Dream* Overture has a very difficult opening, though it sounds easy enough. In my own recording of it some of the chords are pretty good, but if you listen carefully you'll notice that, to start with, the two flutes are not together, and also that the fourth chord is not quite neat.

I am often asked what happens at the rehearsal of a concerto if soloist and conductor disagree. Well, some unpleasant things have happened sometimes, but I, personally, and I think most conductors, do their best to sink their feelings in order to give the soloist as free a hand as possible. I have had some interesting preliminary rehearsals with soloists before meeting the orchestra, and I think that orchestras like to change their style of playing to conform with that of different soloists, if they are properly prepared by a conductor who has already made himself familiar with the soloist's wishes.

Certain types of romantic concerto put a big responsibility on the conductor. The soloist may be doing all sorts of things with the time and yet the conductor has got to indicate the beats, however irregular they may be, with absolute clarity or the orchestra will not be together. It's particularly hard for the conductor when a solo pianist or violinist has a rushing scale passage and the orchestra has to come in exactly at the top of the scale.

I'm sometimes asked why the orchestra never seems to look at the conductor. Actually, of course, players do look up quite a lot and I find myself put off a bit if I don't meet the eye of a player who is just beginning some important tune, but basically the experienced orchestral player can always see the conductor, even when he is looking at his music, because the music is so placed that the conductor's movements are visible just over the top of the copy.

And so we come to performance. This is a difficult thing to describe, but I feel very strongly that the approach to performance is different from any amount of rehearsal; just as in sport, where the effort of a race or match is quite different from anything that we may do in training. There must be an intensity of a different kind: the work must be lifted, as it were, off its feet — too many performances have their feet firmly planted on solid earth, and that isn't music. Everyone, most of all the conductor, must be concentrating with an intensity that is quite outside daily life. My father used to tell us that Gladstone, ten minutes after a speech had begun, was streaming with perspiration, and seemed to be unconscious of any externals: he was simply pouring his message into the hearts of his audience. And I used to notice an interesting thing with Nikisch: he would come on to the platform sometimes with a streaming cold, coughing and sneezing; he would begin to conduct, and the cold would disappear all through the work, to break out again in the interval. That is the kind of concentration that we all should try and cultivate: if it banishes a cold it must indeed be of the faith that moves mountains. So it is with musical interpretation: it isn't the sound of the music, but the magic of the message conveyed by that sound from the deepest suffering to the triumphant elation of a Beethoven, of a Bach, that can bring a new vision of the world to the man in the street.

THE CONDUCTOR AND POSITION

This short essay is taken from the 1937 reprint of Sir Adrian's *Handbook on the Technique of Conducting*. Much of the material in that small booklet he later amplified and some of those essays we have included in *Boult on Music*.

It has probably occurred to most people that there is a striking difference in the power with which singers are able to get hold of their audience, but few will believe that this is not only a question of personality. As a general rule, the singer who leans back has more difficulty in making good than the singer who leans forward. It feels very well to throw your chest out and your shoulders back in order to breathe freely, but this can really be done better when the weight of the body is on the front part of the foot and not on the heel. The motive power of the song is thus directed straight at the audience, whereas the singer who leans back throws his weight upwards and over the heads of the majority of his hearers sitting in the stalls.

This exactly applies to conducting. Your players are usually below your hand and you cannot get hold of them unless you lean towards them, taking care to keep the head up and shoulders back, in order to avoid a crouching attitude. With a chorus the matter is different, but it is perfectly possible to conduct a chorus high above you and yet lean forward, or even stand on the toes, though this is not necessary. Indeed, Sir Henry Wood has been kind enough to suggest that a warning should be added here against too much standing on the toes. It is apt to bring on cramp during a long day's rehearsal.

Another thing to guard against is the foolish-looking habit of 'giving' at the knees. It is easy to get a feeling that

extra emphasis is put into a down-beat by a slight loosening at
the knee, but a glance at anyone who does this will put an end
to this belief. The same can also be said of the habit of walking
about while conducting. An occasional movement may do no
harm, but the less of this the better.

It is well for conductors to bear in mind what may be
aptly called the Line of Sight. This is rarely a straight line, but
it should never be bent too far from the straight. It runs from
the conductor's eye to the point of his stick and on to the eye of
the particular player or the central or chief person of the group
he is conducting.

Before leaving the question of position, it would be well
for a conductor to find at once a comfortable Rest Position,
that is to say, a position in which he waits for silence before
beginning a performance, which is also somewhere near the
centre of his movements in conducting. The hand should be a
short distance above the desk, which should not be high
enough to interfere with easy movement, but can be used
sometimes as a support for the hand, and should be in a
convenient position for counting out empty bars when accompanying songs and concertos. The Line of Sight and the Rest
Position should be bent downwards, though not too much so,
in the middle. That is to say, the point of the stick should find
itself not far below a line drawn from the eye of the conductor
to the eye of the player sitting immediately in front of him.
The Rest Position is not immovable: for instance, at the
begining of a work involving only a part of the orchestra, say,
the first violins, both the Line of Sight and the Rest Position
are turned towards them.

PREPARING NEW MUSIC

The following talk on preparing an unfamiliar score for performance was broadcast on the Home Service in July 1944.

It is obvious that in musical interpretation the most important
thing is to catch the attention and interest of the listener at the
outset and hold them to the last bar. It is, therefore, of

first-class importance that the performer should base his knowledge of the work in hand with a clear picture of its shape and flow, and this from a number of points of view. It is, I think, necessary that he should clearly see the rise and fall of emotional intensity throughout the work, noting the peaks and valleys and their relative height and depth. It is equally necessary that he should see how the work passes through its different keys. One can perhaps compare it with going out for a walk from the environment of one's own home out through strange country and coming gradually back to the country (or key) that one knows. The third aspect is that of the musical themes used by the composer. The would-be performer must get a sense of the sequence in which these themes are used, of their interplay, their contrast and their balance one to another.

Now it seems to me that the best way to get this kind of bird's-eye view of a work in these different aspects is to read it through, several times if necessary, at a very fast pace, considerably faster than the pace at which one ultimately intends to perform it. All this means that one is able to see it, as it were, from a distance and get, if possible, a sense of the work being printed on two pages of an enormous book in such a way that from the first bar to the last it all comes into a single field of sight.

Once this picture has been grasped, at any rate fairly clearly, we can then afford to spend time examining the details. After we have looked at a fine view from a hilltop for some minutes, we are then ready to make use of a telescope and explore details of the landscape, but all the time the picture as a whole should be kept in mind. In this way, the music becomes part of ourselves and we can concentrate on its performance with vigour and confidence, so that the listener is able to grasp the work in one piece, and even at a first hearing will feel how it unfolds inevitably from the start to finish.

May I suggest that a large number of music lovers deprive themselves of a great source of pleasure by making up their minds that they are quite incapable of reading music away from an instrument? This armchair enjoyment of music is nothing like so difficult to learn as it might appear. If you give a few minutes a day to it and start with a well-known

hymn tune or pianoforte piece and gradually bring yourself to
things you know less well and things that are more complicated, you will be surprised how quickly the notes will convey
their sounds to you and give you pleasure. At the same time
you might take a miniature score of your favourite orchestral
work, particularly if it is one of the classical period, and follow
with it at a concert. You will very soon find that if you care to
spend a few minutes with that score in your armchair soon
after the performance, many pages of it will convey their
meaning to you.

I think it is not too much to say that no one, whether
amateur or professional, who hopes to play or sing to others in
a way which will give them the pleasure and inspiration that
great music can bring us when well performed, can really
hope to make a successful job of it unless they have this power
of reading the printed page and getting a quick mental
picture, such as I have described, before they begin the
detailed study of a work.

Having studied the score one now has to think how to
make it possible at rehearsal for the orchestra to absorb this
knowledge in the quickest possible way. As I've been stressing
the advantages of getting an overall view of the work at the
outset, it's obvious that I must begin by conveying this to the
orchestra, and so I always play the work straight through to
start with, and go into detail afterwards.

Talking About Conducting

In 1947 Sir Adrian gave this interview for *The Conductor*, the
official journal of the National Association of Brass Band
Conductors.

Q: Memory plays an important part in a conductor's make-
up. How best can a good memory be acquired?

ACB: I have a feeling that the question of memory has not by
any means been fully covered yet, and I should very much like
to see a new book issued which will gather up the methods and

theories of a number of experts, and perhaps give some idea of
their relative importance. Miss Lilias Mackinnon has issued
two excellent little books published by the Oxford University
Press.[1] There is a great deal of valuable information in them,
and they cover a good deal of ground, but to take one example
Miss Mackinnon, although she mentions the methods of
ocular photography, treats it as one of a number of methods,
whereas Mr. Edward Maryon, whose Marcotone System has
unfortunately not found its way into print, believes that this is
the only way to memorise properly — in fact, he goes so far as
to say that the eye itself will gradually take over the functions
of a camera. The interesting part of his method is that one is
simply not allowed to hear the sound of the music while one is
studying, nor is one allowed to analyse in any way, or
compare passages. They must be photographed first simply as
symbols on the page, and their musical meaning will come
later. I have only recently studied Mr. Maryon's method, and
I am bound to say it produces surprising results. It is, of
course, very difficult for a trained musician to look at a page of
music without hearing its sound, but I think I have now been
able to establish my agreement with Mr. Maryon's view, and
that a photography of the bar symbols without thought of
their meaning does impress itself on the memory in a quite
extraordinary way.

There is no doubt that the process of memorising is an
entirely different thing for young people and for those of
middle age. The whole thing is much easier when you are
young, and I think that one can very easily impress on one's
mind the full sound of music in the early twenties, whereas as
one gets older this become more difficult, and one has to
associate it with the picture of the symbols, and also with the
sight of the key-board fingering and so on.

No doubt everybody must find their own way, but I
would certainly suggest that the visual side of it should not be
forgotten.

Q: Have you a preference for any particular type of baton?

---

[1]*Musical Secrets*, O.U.P., London, 1936; *Music by Heart*, O.U.P., London,
1938.

ACB: I think the answer to this question lies really in the shape of the conductor's hand and the size of his fingers. One cannot make a hard and fast rule. The important thing is that the stick should be a really live instrument (I had almost said limb) in the hands of the conductor, and that the point of the stick should be the centre of interest and the magnet of the eyes of all those he is conducting. I would suggest to my colleagues that when they watch other conductors, they should give a thought as to whether their eyes are not really more attracted by the hand of the conductor than by the point of his stick. I am afraid this will be found to be the case with very many, and that being so, why on earth do they bother with a stick at all?

Seriously, of course, a stick — particularly if it is white enamel, rather than the dead kind of varnished wood colour which one so often sees — can be a much more lively thing for a band to look at than the most expressive hand, and, further, the stick if properly held will enable a great deal more to be said than if the hand were waved about. The human hand can remain quite still while it is guiding a stick through the air and covering a considerable amount of space, but the fingers and wrist must be very loose in order to do it, thus saving a great deal of energy.

I therefore find that my large hand and thick fingers hold most comfortably a stick that has a fairly fat handle. A very thin handle may be all right for those with very small hands. We have said that the stick itself must be white. White enamel is best, but many of us whose hands incline to be damp cannot hold this kind of wooden surface, and I personally find I need to have a cork handle, which I can keep clean with sand-paper — or to have the handle covered with one or two elastic bands, which enable me to keep comfortably my hold on the stick without tightening or stiffening, which I certainly do when I have to hold pure wood. This, of course, stiffens the beat, and may lead to muscular and nervous troubles in the arm.

I am told that my stick is 21½ inches long, and I have already said that if a stick is not properly used, it should be left at home. This does not mean to imply that I prefer to use no stick, or that I think it is a good thing, except possibly where little groups of eight or ten players or singers are concerned. For more than this, as I say, a white stick is much the easiest thing to see, and provided that it is loosely and freely worked it is the most expressive instrument you can find.

Q: What is your method of rehearsing a new work. Do you play it straight through or stop for errors?

ACB: I think it is very important that the players should get as clear a picture at once of the work as a whole; its rise and fall to and from its climaxes, and its general make-up. The reason for this is that the audience also should be introduced at a first hearing to this idea of the work as one piece, moving in some direction, and not just a haphazard collection of more (or less) agreeable sounds. If the audience have got to get this, the players have got to get it, and it is the conductor who has to give it to them — and so please, Mr. Conductor, let your players struggle through without stopping if possible, perhaps even more than once, before you begin picking out the difficult passages and getting them perfect. There is another aspect to this, that players always wish to improve, and if at one rehearsal you play straight through a work and give them some general idea of it, you may with any luck find that at the next rehearsal a good many of them have found opportunities for a little private practice, and the work automatically goes a good deal better, before one has had to go in for the trouble and friction of pulling passages to pieces, and getting detailed perfection.

Q: Do you employ any difference in your techniques when conducting larger groups, such as choral bodies?

ACB: I always like to think that the space in which the point of my stick moves is roughly determined by an imaginary piece of elastic, which is fastened to my eye at one end, the eye of the central player or a singer at the other, and in the middle is attached to the point of my stick. The stick stretches the elastic, but it should always be pulled back to that central point. Now I think it follows that if there is a large group in front of me the elastic will more often be stretched a bit further, particularly if something has to be covered on one of the wings, but the main movement of the stick should always be the middle of the space.

Q: Do you believe in praising an orchestra after a particularly successful rehearsal or performance?

ACB: Yes, certainly. In rehearsal particularly I think it is important that the players should know when they have done the thing to the conductor's liking — in fact, it is just as important as a necessary correction. I often see a conductor in rehearsal correcting something and then leaving it, as if it was at any rate an improvement and bearable, but not really very good. After a performance one has not the same opportunity, but now and then I think it is right that an opportunity should be found at a subsequent rehearsal of pointing out any high spot in the work of the players.

Q: Many band conductors who are no longer young have not had the advantage of academic training. How could they best improve their musicianship?

ACB: It is an astonishment to me whenever I have the pleasure of seeing something of the band world that such wonderful and beautiful results can so often be achieved by band conductors who have had no musical training whatever — in the wider sense — and who, from the nature of their lives can only give a very small part of each week even to thinking about music. It only shows what an inherently musical nation we are, and I don't think that a finer proof of this could possibly be found than the brass band movement as a whole. But this is not answering the question, and if any of my brass band colleagues would like some suggestions, I think perhaps the best thing that those with very limited spare time can do is to hear others at work, preferably in the flesh, but also by listening on the wireless, or on a gramophone record of a fine orchestral performance of a work one is studying for brass band. This should help a great deal. I have many happy recollections of how a wonderful new light has come to a work which I thought I knew well when I have heard a very fine performance of it.

The next thing that I would advise is reading — on the right lines, of course, because everyone's time is precious nowadays. Composers' lives may give a light on some of their compositions which will act as a refreshment the next time one conducts it. Books about music — some of them are most helpful. Perhaps for a newcomer to musical literature Dr. Percy Scholes' books will be as useful as any that could be found. It may be that our conductor has a special interest in any one instrument. Well, perhaps occasionally he can join in chamber music, or an orchestral performance, or play an instrument in somebody else's band — or perhaps sing in a choral society. All these things will give a new direction to one's thought on music and are heartily to be recommended. Wireless and gramophone are accessible to most people now, and it would seem to be an easy matter for conductors who can spare the time to widen their knowledge by this means.

Q: Are you a firm believer in conducting without the copy when possible?

ACB: There is no doubt at all that when the score is in your head there is no longer any need for your head to be in the score, and that means a higher pitch of concentration and a better performance; but the ostentatious removal of the conductor's desk has no necessary part in this, and it is very much better to have the desk always before you, and the copy on it even if you forget to turn over.

Q: Are you favourable to a minimum amount of 'presentation' in respect of an orchestral performance, such as a subdued light in the auditorium, a strong light on the orchestra and conductor?

ACB: I have always been strongly of the view that the conductor's appeal is to the eyes of his orchestra only, and to the ears of his audience. I know that some conductors consider that it is their duty to indicate to the audience what instruments in the orchestra are at the moment playing the part of most importance. Personally I think this is absolute nonsense, and I cannot feel that any fading of lights, once the orchestra can see their music and the point of the conductor's stick, is going to do anything to help the music, which after all is what the audience has paid to hear.

Q: What style of beat do you employ in order to get a broad flowing effect?

ACB: I am inclined to think that we conductors are all rather apt to make our gestures of the nature of an up- or down-beat, and that a broad horizontal sweep from left to right can very much help our players to get the kind of playing which the terms *legato* and *sostenuto* best describe. I think we are all inclined to forget that, although when asked about it we should no doubt agree that the type of beat has its instant effect on the players, and that we are giving them an additional difficulty if we ask them to play a smooth, flowing tune when they are looking at a sharp, jerky, little beat.

THE ART OF CONDUCTING

The next five talks were broadcast as a series early in 1960 and printed in *The Listener*.

I. The Art of Rehearsal

I often wonder what our audiences think about the matter of preparation for an orchestral concert. I daresay that it is not generally realised that, though a short studio concert of fairly familiar music may be rehearsed only once, the usual B.B.C. Symphony Concert usually needs three rehearsals of three hours each, and may have as many as six. I have been concerned with two opera performances recently, Busoni's *Doktor Faust* at the Festival Hall, and a recording of Vaughan Williams' *Pilgrim's Progress* for the B.B.C. (to be broadcast in March or April), and for each of these we had eight rehearsals.

Planning a rehearsal is a personal thing, and, with the greatest respect, I often feel that some of my most distinguished colleagues waste a tremendous amount of time and energy — their own energy, as well as that of their chorus, orchestra and soloists — by starting at the beginning of the first rehearsal, and insisting on a perfect performance of the first few bars before they proceed any further. There are some who will never allow the slightest blemish to pass without stopping the music, pointing out what was wrong (even if the error is obvious to everyone in the room), and starting again some little way back.

We had a very eminent visitor at the B.B.C. in pre-war days, who never gave the orchestra a chance of playing the work straight through and getting a picture of it as a whole until the actual performance. One of the players told me that he didn't think that they had ever been allowed to play more than ten bars at a stretch, without being pulled up for something.

Some conductors seem to be afraid that if they let a mistake pass without instantly stopping and commenting on it, the orchestra will think that they have scored off the conductor, and will boast that they got away with something 'the old man didn't notice'.

This painstaking and meticulous method may perhaps be right and necessary with the more unsophisticated players of Southern Europe. It was the early method of Toscanini, and of others of the greatest conductors of their time, but it is undeniable that it uses up an enormous amount of rehearsal time, and is quite fatal for the quick rehearsing that so often is forced on us in this country by economic necessity.

I, personally, would go far further, and say that besides wasting time it is, from the psychological standpoint, an absolutely wrong approach to Anglo-Saxon professionals and, I might add, to Northern Europeans generally, as far as my experience goes.

We Britishers have most of us experience of playing games, and being led, and if driven from the first bar of the first rehearsal through a series of three or four rehearsals, will certainly lose interest long before the concert, and find it very difficult to recapture our freshness and come up to concert pitch even when we see the audience in the hall or the red light in the studio. Our people like to be led and not driven. Like the trainer of a team or a racing crew we increase the tension as we go along, but our final rehearsal is still a preparation for the concert, and in no way a reproduction of it.

In other words: some conductors conduct a concert at

every rehearsal, and we others like to build the whole thing up gradually to concert pitch. It was interesting to see how even Toscanini, working with the British orchestra, realised that with the utmost willingness, they could not give him his maximum tension before the great day. Nikisch, on the other hand, from whom I learnt so much by attending his rehearsals many years ago, seemed to approach his rehearsals from the easiest possible point of view. He would start by going straight through a work, or a large section of it, and he would then go through it again, perhaps skipping passages that had gone well at the first reading, but dipping into the places that needed hard work, and giving them hard work, but never losing sight of the fact that it was a rehearsal and not a performance.

His object seemed to be to improve the whole thing gradually within the rehearsal time at his disposal, but not necessarily aiming at a positive ideal performance. He would often touch up a salient passage, and when that was right, leave it to the players to apply what he had done to other passages which might be similar.

The longer I live and work, the more strongly I respect the players with whom I am privileged to make music. After a preliminary run-through one often finds that at the second approach the things that one might have stopped and talked about have all corrected themselves through the skill and judgment of the players. We conductors *all* talk much too much!

II. Is a Conductor Really Necessary?

I am often asked this question, though it is sometimes wrapped up a little more politely. As our bread and butter depends on it, I suppose people hardly expect to get a perfectly honest reply!

I think it is clear that an ensemble performance of music, whether it consists of three people or a hundred, needs a directing mind if it is going to be really worth listening to, and it is important that that direction should not intrude on the performance and be audible at it: it must confine itself to rehearsals. I expect most of us can remember string quartet performances where the first violin dominated everything, and relegated the rest of the quartet to the status of an accompaniment — and, of course, many light combinations are directed by a pianist-conductor or violinist-conductor, who drags the (usually ill-rehearsed) show along in a very obvious way, in marked contrast to the charming performances which one can sometimes hear from that medium.

Who, then, is to do that directing? Time was when the director was a pianist, an organist, a violinist, a composer with a club which he banged on the floor (or on his foot as poor Lully found out), and I can myself remember in an important South European capital a man who helped the conductor at the Royal Opera House by striking up on a wooden clapper the moment the chorus began, and going on all the time they were singing. The silent conductor came in in the early nineteenth century, and seems to be a fixture for the present. He can have an uncanny influence over the players and singers, and sometimes, when several conductors are sharing a concert, it is quite extraordinary to hear the difference in tonal quality as the conductors change places.

What does the conductor do? I am sometimes told that the players don't ever look at me. Of course they don't; they have to look at their music and read it as they go along. It is my business to try and see that an eloquent stick is seen by the player just over the music which he is reading — the eye can take in a wide area round the spot at which one is actually looking. It is very important that the player should place his music so that he can see the stick just over it. It is also the conductor's business to see that his stick is inside the field of the players' vision, and I would humbly suggest that if the conductor waves his hand and stick round in the air well over his head, it is not so easy to see as it would be just in front of him. With a choir ranged above him, the conductor will, of course, have to move in a larger and higher circle, but again, I try and see that singers keep their music well up so that the stick can be seen just above it, as with the orchestra. At the same time, a chorus has usually had the benefit of a good deal more rehearsal than the orchestra, and, of course, the singers must form the habit of paying attention to the beat, when concert time comes, as well as in the later stages of rehearsal; but prior to that I'm not at all sure that they should be conducted at all. They should look at their copies while learning their notes, and I used often to sit at the pianoforte myself during these early stages, for it can only do harm if you conduct them when they aren't ready to look at the beat.

The conductor, then, has the task of leading the ensemble wherever there is a start, a finish, a pause, or a change of time or pace. He is the mainspring of the emotional interpretation of the work, and must often lead by anticipation. His view of the work as a whole must never be obscured, but must pass to the audience in order that the flow and inevitable forward movement of the music should never seem to falter. Now, in classical music there are often long passages of slow but relentless advance which in themselves call for no special action from the conductor. Here, we are told, Mendelssohn would cease to beat altogether, and Wagner would take a pinch of snuff. Nobody ever seems to stop conducting nowadays, but I wonder whether it wouldn't be a good thing sometimes. At any rate, I can often feel an over-heavy accentuation and stodginess when a conductor insists on going on with a heavy up-and-down movement all through these passages. Players and singers cannot be expected to perform with deftness and delicacy if they see their director behaving like a windmill, and, in fact, conducting *fortissimo* when he expects the performance to be *pianissimo*.

When talking about rehearsals the other day I said that I was coming more and more to respect and trust the players with whom I work — they will usually put things right for themselves (as soon as they know how the interpreter's mind works) without being told how to do it in meticulous detail; nor indeed do they want exaggerated gestures. I think back to the technique of Arthur Nikisch: a stick of shining white that could readily be seen by everyone, actuated with the utmost restraint mostly by the thumb and two fingers, yet in a way that conveyed the pace and emotion of the music to perfection. *Legato, staccato,* expression of the widest range, could all be shown by the way the point of the stick would move. Behind the fingers was the wrist, and (rarely) the elbow to indicate the broader and louder effects. The shoulder never moved.

The left hand amplified the right at the rare moments when the stick could not express all he wished; but there was never that dual looking-glass action that we see so often nowadays when left and right arms do exactly the same thing together, and the players must surely wonder what part of the conductor's anatomy they are expected to look to for guidance.

I have said before that we conductors all talk too much. Now I add: we all *do* too much also — but I still maintain that we must be there to do something!

III. Conducting Concertos

I have a feeling that many conductors (and orchestras) are inclined to think that a concerto is a somewhat unwelcome interruption to a concert, stuck in just to help the box office, and needing an unfair amount of rehearsal time, because nearly every soloist in the world wants to play through every note of the concerto on the day of the concert, even if he or she has played it the day before.

I am afraid I don't agree at all. A programme consisting of three string quartets (or two, if they are long ones) may be perfect and, likewise, a series of two or three symphonies can give us a memorable evening; but the average orchestral concert can gain very much from the contrast of a fine concerto finely performed.

There is a great danger, however, that orchestra and conductor will want to rattle through the concerto at the end of the rehearsal without giving the poor soloist a chance to say whether he wants anything special, or any kind of tempo that isn't the obvious standard way of playing the thing. He must just give one more average performance, poor creature.

Personally I daresay I overdo it, but whenever possible I meet the soloist beforehand and give him a chance to tell me exactly what he wants. This may sometimes involve a word or two to the orchestra before the actual rehearsal of the concerto, but it seems to me the only fair way of handling the whole thing. A very keen listener in my B.B.C. days once said he was always amused to hear the differences we used to make in the introductory ritornello of a concerto, to conform with what the soloist was going to do later in the movement.

One sometimes hears stories of concerto performances at which conductor and soloist have agreed to differ, and the soloist has his way in the solos, but at every *tutti* the orchestra would jump forward, or drag backwards, and maintain this change until the next solo entry. This is a nice way to present a great classic to a long-suffering audience. Sheer sportsmanship surely should allow the soloist to have his way for half-an-hour when the conductor is unquestioned boss for the rest of the concert. I think it may usually be assumed that the soloist has spent 100 hours practising and thinking about the concerto to every one spent by the conductor, so presumably the soloist does know best.

At this point, it might be amusing to recount an experience of mine which is, I think, the most extreme example in my memory of a difference with a soloist. In the early years of the B.B.C. Symphony Orchestra we always offered our soloists two rehearsals, the first with pianoforte or with orchestra, as he wished. The second was, of course, with orchestra, but on this occasion Gieseking, whose visits were always looked forward to by us all with great pleasure, arrived literally at the eleventh hour on the morning of the concert. He had been playing in Holland the night before. He came on to the platform of the old Queen's Hall, and looked with horror at the assembled array of something like seventy string players waiting to play the Bach D minor, which I had always looked on, and played with others, as a vigorous open-air kind of piece. I told him that the players did know how to accompany, and suggested we should try a movement and see what he thought. At the end of the movement he still thought there were too many, and though the balance engineer and I both assured him that the tone of the pianoforte showed clearly above the strings, he said he found the texture was wrong. The word 'texture' struck me, and I said: 'Mr. Gieseking, are you really thinking of this as a pianoforte concerto, or one with a harpsichord?' He jumped at once and said, 'Yes, yes, the 'arpsichord'. So I said, 'Then why do you play it on a great concert grand piano?' 'Oh, the piano, it is there, I must play it, but I think of the 'arpsichord all the time.' I thereupon sent about fifty of the Orchestra home at once, and the other twenty stayed and tinkled through the Concerto as if we were in my lady's boudoir. He asked me afterwards whether I hadn't liked it so, and I had to confess that I had always thought this Concerto a more robust work, but that I was very happy that our audience and listeners should have the opportunity of hearing a different point of view. Gieseking was a very great pianist indeed, and his conception, though different from the one usually held, was logical and may well have been nearer to the performances which Bach himself gave.

I'm afraid I am rather a rebel about the feeling that people seem to have, that if an orchestral accompaniment is too strong, the removal of a few strings will improve matters. I can't agree; you may get a clearer picture of the woodwind if you do this, but you will certainly have too much brass, unless you warn the players very firmly, and if it is a violin concerto you will be bringing your *tutti* violin tone that much nearer to a solo quality. Provided that they play quietly, the contrast will be greater, and the tone more beautiful the greater the number of players taking part. Berlioz has said that one instrument alone can be beautiful; two, playing the same tune, far less so, but after that as the number increases, the beauty also can increase, and I would add that this is true both in *pianissimo* and *fortissimo*: the more people you have playing the same tune, the more beautiful it is, whether loud or soft.

As for piano concertos, in this country, and I believe nowhere else, the conductor often stands between the pianoforte and the audience. This is to me a poisonous position: one can hear only the soloist; the orchestra behind that lid blaze away without the conductor hearing them at all, and the lid gets terribly in the way of the actual conducting and control of the orchestra. A so-called improvement is sometimes effected by a shortening of the stick which holds the lid in place — a criminal thing to do: the pianoforte manufacturer has calculated the angle at which the lid should be held in order that the sound can be produced straight out into the hall. A shortened stick alters this angle of direction, and throws the sound straight down at the feet of the people sitting in the front row, and the poor player's tone is correspondingly weakened.

It is a long time since I decided once and for all that Continental and American conductors were right, and no conductor should place himself between the pianoforte and the audience. I was conducting in Leicester when the soloist was Sir Malcolm Sargent. We had had what we thought was a spanking rehearsal of the Second Rachmaninov and had dispersed for tea when a friend who had been sitting in the hall came up and said, 'I hope you don't mind my saying I have heard very little of the piano this afternoon'. From that moment I determined always to stand between the instrument and the orchestra, so that I could hear the accompaniment, and not only the soloist. If one turns sideways, one is wonderfully close to the keyboard, and if one keeps the right hand and arm well out to the right everybody can see the stick. I am often asked why I do this by people who have not been abroad much, so there is the reason!

IV. Arranging Orchestras

Concert halls throughout the world vary a great deal in their platforms, and orchestral tradition varies considerably also, so that a touring orchestra has many and unusual problems to solve every time it moves to a new hall. There are many principles involved, and it is true to say that there is no perfect solution to all the problems at once. Indeed, I have heard it said that the right plan would be to let everyone sit where he wishes, regardless of the instrument he is playing — a better ensemble might be achieved that way, and there would be no blocks of homogeneous sound. But the disadvantages would also be formidable, and I personally am not inclined to try this bold plan, exciting though the results might be!

But we might explore some of the principles and discuss the various solutions though we certainly shall not be able to agree on the perfect answers. First, are we going to place our players on a level stage or on the tiers and steps which are built into most British halls? I prefer the levels to be different: the strings outnumber the woodwind by six or more to one, and it seems only sensible that the eight, twelve, or even sixteen woodwind players should be raised: they have much solo work to do. On the other hand their instruments have a greater penetrating power than the strings, and string players must often be encouraged to listen to a wind soloist as they make their contribution to the accompanying background.

The only two rules that are in almost universal observance in the orchestral world are: first, that the leader of the orchestra sits on the conductor's immediate left; and, second, that the group of woodwind soloists sits in the middle of the platform with the first players in the middle, flute next to oboe sitting on the first rise, and clarinet and bassoon together behind, in the middle of the second rise. But in some halls this is impossible, because the first rise is so far forward that there is hardly any room for the strings: in this case the woodwind must sit higher and further back. In other halls the level space is so wide that it throws the woodwind group too far back. This is a nuisance because their tone can easily be submerged, particularly in a theatre where the proscenium arch comes down low and throws the orchestral sound straight upwards instead of outwards to the audience. However, it is sometimes possible to get boxes and build the woodwind forward a bit.

By way of exception, in a provincial hall recently I saw the whole woodwind chorus placed in front of the platform to the conductor's right. This might give some distortion to those sitting in front seats in the hall, but to me in a distant gallery the result was often most effective.

Having placed the woodwind, we should then see how far the strings can be packed in. In placing them it is now the fashion to start at the left with the first violins, and radiate round, second violins next, violas, then 'cellos, with the double basses on the extreme right of the platform, sometimes in front, sometimes further back, according to the space available.

There are two things here which I dislike intensely. This plan puts all the treble on the left of the platform and all the bass on the right, and, I submit, gives the audience a most unbalanced picture of the orchestral sound. Those sitting on the right of the hall (facing the platform) will get a preponderance of bass; in fact, in the Royal Festival Hall, if one sits on that side one hears the bass sound first, and the tunes trickle across the hall a fraction late.

In Vienna, in one of the most perfect concert halls in the world, the basses are always placed in a row across the back of the top stage. They have the organ case immediately behind them, and a splendid foundation to the whole texture comes forward. The same layout is possible in the Royal Festival Hall, and I much prefer it that way.

This principle of tonal balance also affects the position of the second violins, about which I feel most strongly, although I am in a small minority. However, on my side are Bruno Walter, Monteux, Klemperer, and a few others, including Toscanini, who was adamant about it and insisted that the string balance should be preserved by placing the second violins on his right, exactly balancing the firsts on his left. The seconds thus share the front of the platform instead of being tucked away behind the firsts, where, I maintain, their tone is largely lost. Indeed, the practice which I so dislike came in only about fifty years ago, and I am sure that the shades of Richter, Weingartner, Nikisch, and Toscanini are frowning at the modern idea, which thinks only of the convenience of the performers and nothing of the effect on the audience as envisaged by the composer.

True, it is easier for the first violins to have the seconds near them, and for the violas to be placed between the seconds and the 'cellos, but is ease of playing and convenience to be the chief criterion? Surely the result is what matters, and I can assert that on many occasions in many halls I have heard the give-and-take answering passages, which occur in all music from Mozart to the present day, sound completely ineffective when the answer comes as a pale reflection from behind the first violins instead of springing up bravely from the opposite side of the platform. If it is true, as is sometimes said, that the second violins are so far turned away from the audience that they cannot be heard, I will flatly contradict; it is not so. If the outside players turn inwards and put their shoulders between their instruments and the audience, they can easily be stopped by the conductor. Another argument, that the firsts and seconds often play in octaves or unison, bow together, and therefore should sit together, is to me unimportant. If the leader of the seconds is any use, he will secure a perfect ensemble; if there is a pianoforte on the platform it does make it more difficult for him, but not impossible, and there is no doubt that a long unison, like the slow movement of *Sheherazade*, was thought of by Rimsky-Korsakov as coming from the front of the whole width of the stage in a most telling way.

Incidentally, the space each string player needs to enable him to bow comfortably varies a good deal. The famous Amsterdam Concertgebouw Orchestra has always placed itself exceedingly close, thereby helping its wonderful ensemble.

There are not so many considerations in regard to the placing of brass and percussion, once the strings and woodwind are settled. It must not be forgotten that the sound of a horn emerges from behind the player's elbow. In the Royal Festival Hall, if the horn group is placed too near the wooden fence which separates the orchestra from the chorus seats, their tone hits the boarding behind them and is curiously magnified. The brass is often divided, with horns to one side of the woodwind, and trumpets and trombones to the other. I like the trombones in the Festival Hall to be placed a little sideways so that they play into the orchestra and not directly out to the audience. Their tone blends better that way. Percussion, harps and celesta fit in where they can, but I like the percussion as near the middle as possible, particularly the timpani which, like the string basses, seem so often to be the foundation of the whole.

In choral music, particularly where the soloists are closely involved in the choral texture, they are sometimes placed in front of the chorus nowadays, above and behind the orchestra. When the front of the platform is very low, it is indeed often better for most of the audience to have the solo quartet near the chorus; the orchestra, of course, must keep their accompaniment discreet. Once again I say, as on previous occasions: trust the orchestra. They can actually hear the soloists, and judge the balance for themselves, far more easily than if the soloists are singing away from them with their backs turned.

V. The Conductor:
Foreground or Background?

I have recently tried to answer the question: 'Is the conductor really necessary?', and now I want to ask another: 'Does the audience want to look at the conductor?' Or perhaps: 'Has the audience paid to see the conductor, or to hear him?' There are not many conductors whom I would wish to watch for any length of time; indeed, if I want to listen with real concentration, I always shut my eyes; it is astonishing how much more one can hear when one does this. I am sometimes puzzled because people talk about 'seeing a conductor' as if he were a film star. Surely one should say 'hear' about anyone whose job is the interpretation of music. But it is a good idea for members of the choir and orchestra to see the conductor, although when conducting I do not expect them to look at me; they have to see me over the top of the music they are reading. Many years ago I was starting a rehearsal at a country festival, and as the choir stood up, a rather tall friend of mine noticed that there was a short girl in the row behind her, so she said over her shoulder, 'Is it all right; can you see the conductor?' 'Quite all right, miss, thank you', came the brisk reply. 'I saw him last year.' That put the matter into a healthy perspective from my point of view! When I was even younger I asked a distinguished conductor, who died thirty years ago, to give me a lesson. In describing the appropriate gesture at a particular point he said: 'You must indicate to the audience here that a clarinet solo is starting'. I have always thought that the way to do that was to provide the right background of sound for the entry of the solo clarinet, and then leave it to the ears of the audience. But perhaps I am wrong.

The power of a great conductor over an orchestra and choir is immense, and is very difficult to describe in words. Different conductors can have an utterly different influence on the actual tone produced, particularly by the string players, and they can fully exemplify any theories that may be held about the power of thought over collections of human beings. For some years I had the privilege of attending part of the opera festival at Munich in the days when Bruno Walter was

Director there, and a queer thing used to happen in the Wagner Theatre, which was built on the model of Bayreuth, with the orchestra, concealed, playing in a deep pit, and with the conductor also invisible to the audience. The starting drill was always the same: three bells, one minute apart, and after the third bell a gradual darkening of the house lights until nothing was to be seen but the exciting glow that came up from the orchestra pit and threw some light on the curtain. When Bruno Walter himself was conducting there was always an anticipatory hush in the audience by the time the lights had been half lowered, but with every other conductor there was movement and whispering even when it was dark, and this stopped only when the first sound of the overture was heard. With Walter it had stopped well before this, and we had the thrill of Wagner's opening note or chord coming to us out of absolute silence.

Why was this? It may well have been that Walter called the orchestra to a state of tension as the lights were being lowered while the other conductors waited slackly for complete darkness. It was always the same, and showed in an extraordinary way the power of a great man over an audience, even when he was out of sight.

The concealed opera director in Munich and Bayreuth now has his counterpart in the studio conductor at a broadcast or a recording session; he must make his appeal to the ears of his audience through the eyes of the orchestra and chorus. To me it is the right way, and though I occasionally enjoy looking at the technique of a colleague whose work I admire, I do suggest that to shut one's eyes at a concert is the real way to listen.

A matter concerned with performance which worries me a good deal is the tempo not of the separate pieces but of the concert as a whole. Some performers like this tempo to be fast; others prefer it slow. It shows itself principally in two different ways: the inclusion or exclusion of repeats, and the space allowed between the movements of symphonies, sonatas, and quartets. Presumably, composers put the conventional repeat marks into their music because they want the section in question to be played twice. In many cases the shape of the movement as a whole calls for this repetition, although in

some cases the repeat has been put in as a formal matter
without too much thought.

Conductors are particularly inclined to ignore repeats,
except in scherzos, and I cannot see why. The first movements
of all Beethoven Symphonies, except perhaps the Third, call
for the repeat, and seem to me lop-sided without it; and the
finales of Mozart's last three Symphonies assume an utterly
different stature when both repeats are played. Without them,
these finales cannot stand up at all to the greatness of the first
movements, whereas with them the music seems not just twice
as long but ten times as noble and important. I once went to
see Donald Tovey when he was lying ill at his home in
Edinburgh. He had volumes of the great Bach edition all over
him, and on the floor. I said, 'I see you are wallowing in
J.S.B.', and his reply was: 'Yes, it is wonderful, now I'm not
busy, to be able to read them with the repeats'.

Once a movement is over, however, conductors who have
been in too much of a hurry to play the repeats seem to change
their attitude completely: now they would seem to have all the
time in the world. Such different composers as Brahms and
Borodin are often clearly seen to begin, say, a second movement with the final chord of the first still ringing in their ears.
How can the chord ring in one's ears when the audience has
been treated to the spectacle of the conductor mopping his
brow, blowing his nose in some unrelated key, and perhaps
even allowing someone to crash in with some noisy tuning,
with the implication of D minor, when perhaps the movement
has just finished in B flat and is now proceeding to a second
movement in E flat? Surely a symphony, a quartet, or a sonata
is one work, and should be played as such, without interruption between the movements.

PART FOUR

ON OTHER
MUSICIANS

──────────── •◦• ────────────

ERIC BLOM

This tribute to the writer and scholar Eric Blom was broadcast
in the Midlands by the B.B.C. on Blom's death in April 1959.

In the early '20's I found out that the music publishing house
of J. & W. Chester had accumulated a fine music lending
library with a large collection of modern scores. I joined it and
on calling at Great Marlborough Street in London, found it
was in the charge of a gentle young man with a very pleasant
voice and a slight foreign accent, a wide knowledge of music,
and a wonderfully ingenious card index which told him
instantly the whereabouts of all the scores and parts in his
care. I soon found out that his name was Eric Blom, and it
was not long before his erudition found its way into his pen
and he began collaborating with Mrs. Rosa Newmarch in
writing the programme notes for Sir Henry Wood's Concerts.
This was soon followed by notices of important London
concerts in *The Manchester Guardian*, which only stopped when
The Birmingham Post called him to the Midlands in 1931.

He remained in Birmingham for fifteen years, and though
a stern and exacting critic, his work was always constructive.
In the background was the feeling that if the concert hadn't
been as good as usual, well, the City Orchestra was still
Birmingham's own, and still worth supporting. I have known
provincial critics who took the line that they must compare

local effort with the records that they received monthly by
Toscanini or Furtwängler, and say exactly where the local
players fell short — of an orchestra three times the size, and
costing probably ten times as much!

Blom was not that kind, and he saw the Orchestra
through the war difficulties and did not return to London until
1946. By this time he had written a number of books on
various aspects of music, was editing the learned quarterly
Music and Letters, and had assumed a number of important
advisory positions. He was Chairman of the Central Music
Library, a member of the Council of the Royal Musical
Association, of the Music Committee of the British Council,
and was soon to assume the post of principal critic of *The
Observer*. But his greatest work for music was undoubtedly his
editing of the Fifth Edition of *Grove's Dictionary of Music and
Musicians*. This standard work was completely overhauled,
and it is not too much to say that no musical scholar can exist
without it; its nine splendid volumes reflect the greatest credit
on its editor and the hundreds of collaborators he invited to
assist him with articles of all lengths, and dealing with every
aspect of the art.

Eric Blom was a man of modesty and charm and carried
all his great scholarship and erudition as humbly and gently
as anyone I have known. He will be deeply missed among
those who value true scholarship and knowledge, and many
music lovers in Birmingham will remember the slight, modest
figure who always sat in the same seat in the Town Hall,
whose writing they would read with interest, and of whom
they may well be proud even though in his last years his work
had kept them away from them.

THE BUSCH BROTHERS

The following note on Fritz, Adolf and Hermann Busch was
written for the Edinburgh Festival in 1949.

It is now many years since the name of Busch was first heard
in England; it first came to my consciousness — I remember
the night well — when Adolf gave a superb performance of the
Brahms Violin Concerto, with Fritz Steinbach conducting, on
18th March, 1912 in Queen's Hall. These three distinguished
brothers still look so young that it is indeed difficult to realise
their enormous total contribution to music in all countries.
Adolf has given us notable compositions, showing signs of
allegiance to his friend Max Reger (for whose music also I
firmly believe there is still an important future), but at the
moment we think of him as the masterly interpreter, particularly of the classics, and not only as a soloist, but as leader of
the string quartet, partner with Rudolf Serkin, and leader and
director of an unforgettable ensemble, many of whose performances of the greatest classics are happily recorded for our
continual pleasure. Hermann's fine tone and impeccable
musicianship have wonderfully balanced and supported
Adolf's leadership.

Last but not least, Fritz, the eldest brother. One of the
leading conductors of our time, he was chief conductor at
Aachen at the age of twenty-two, has brought lustre to
orchestral performances all over the world, and has been
opera director at Stuttgart and Dresden. He has visited
Britain on a number of occasions.

There was a specially close friendship between Sir
Donald Tovey and all these brothers, whose deep scholarship
and understanding of music naturally endeared them to
Edinburgh's greatest Professor of Music. I shall never forget
the magnificent authority of their performance of the Brahms
Double Concerto, and the Beethoven Triple, with Rudolf
Serkin, in the Usher Hall, on 13th December, 1934. In the
same week, on the introduction of Sir Donald, the Degree of
Doctor of Music was conferred on all three of them together.
It is a very happy occasion that the Festival has now invited
them to come again to Edinburgh, where they have many
friends.

PABLO CASALS

In December 1951, when Casals was seventy-five, Sir Adrian
broadcast this birthday tribute on 'Music Magazine', then on
the B.B.C.'s Home Service.

Surely there are few, if any, public men in the world whose
birthday will be so universally enjoyed, to whom messages
and friendly thoughts will be sent in such large numbers, as
the man who has for more than fifty years been recognised as
the greatest living 'cellist. Indeed, I feel that it is quite
impossible to do justice to the day, and rather than encroach
on the field of the historian or the critic, I would ask your
leave simply to tell some stories of the work I have been
privileged to do with him, and leave you to see the stature of
the man as it may emerge.

   The first time I conducted for Casals was in Liverpool. It
was also the first time I had conducted for a great international artist, so I was naturally thrilled and a bit frightened at the
prospect. I arranged for ninety minutes' rehearsal to be
devoted to the concerto, and told him so. It was the Schumann. We started by playing through to the first *tutti* when
he stopped and said, 'You did say we had time to work? Or
must we just play through?' I repeated my promise of ninety
minutes, and with a grunt of satisfaction he started giving us
all a priceless lesson on every aspect of the passage we had just
played. In this way we went right through the Concerto,
taking just about our ninety minutes, during which I was
silent, except for occasional repetitions of his instructions in
case they had not been fully heard. I was told afterwards that
a worthy committee man had pronounced that 'young Boult
couldn't be much good if he let that 'cello feller do all the
talking'. It was all wonderful, but most wonderful of all was
the slow movement, when I felt the whole direction (at the
performance, too) was gently taken from my hands, and given
back when the last movement began. A curious thing happened a few weeks later when Casals had played the work in
London. Next day we were discussing the performance over
the Professors' lunch table at the Royal College of Music, and
one of my colleagues said, 'You know I felt in the slow

movement that that *pianissimo* in the orchestra was Casals'
and didn't belong to the conductor at all'.

In the Artists' Room at Liverpool Casals had shown me
some programmes of the concerts he was conducting in
Barcelona with a new orchestra he had collected. They were of
great interest, ranging from Bach and the classics to
Tchaikovsky, Debussy and Enescu, whom he considered to be
beside Tovey as one of the greatest living musical thinkers and
the most complete musical phenomenon since Mozart.

He told me he was to have another season the following
May, and I determined to go there, and learn all I could.
Unfortunately he rehearsed in Catalan instead of Spanish,
which I had been frantically trying to learn, but the ample
rehearsal time (I remember he took eight hours over the
Schubert Great C major) made it always easy to see his ideals,
and his method. The orchestra was led by his brother, and
was collected from theatres and cafes, and patiently drilled
into the symphonic style by this great musician and great
teacher.

His regular visits to London in my B.B.C. days gave us
many thrilling experiences in concertos with him, and we
mustn't forget that he took the trouble to include the Elgar
and the monumental work written for him by Donald Tovey,
for which he has a great affection. I remember, too, a
charming occasion when he received the Gold Medal of the
Worshipful Company of Musicians at a lunch given in his
honour, and his speech of thanks showed the simplicity of true
greatness; and just before 'the lights went out over Europe' in
1939 we met at the Lucerne Festival.

When he came again after the war we were invited to
record the Haydn and the Elgar with him. Alas, we had only
time for two movements of the Haydn, and I long for a chance
of finishing it, but the Elgar has been published, and the
records show for themselves the enormous care and trouble
that he took over it all. He was never satisfied, and while
continually chatting with the players round him, he went on
practising the whole time, and hearing and re-hearing the
play-backs until he could bear to think of them as a permanent record. But he could relax, and when a solemn official
emerged from the Listening Room after a test, and said, 'Mr.

Casals, I'm afraid we can hear you singing as you play', he retorted instantly, 'Good, then you can charge double for the records'.

FRITZ KREISLER

Sir Adrian broadcast this tribute to Fritz Kreisler shortly after the violinist's death in January 1962.

When Kreisler first took up the Beethoven Violin Concerto it is no exaggeration to say that everybody played one of the two cadenzas that had been written for it by Josef Joachim. Kreisler as a young man of enormous technical power felt he would like something more exciting with which to show his paces. He therefore composed an entirely new cadenza, including a wonderful passage which combines the two main themes of the first movement.

When I first came to London at the beginning of the century and was given a season ticket for Sir Henry Wood's Sunday and Symphony Concerts, Kreisler played here often. He was bracketed, I think, in most people's minds with Eugène Ysaÿe as leader of his profession, and while some people felt that Ysaÿe's tone was broader and more telling, there were many for whom Kreisler's style in the great classics put him ahead of his rival.

Kreisler and Ysaÿe were great friends, and I remember an old friend of mine, a Dutchman who had settled in Liverpool and for many years was the dominating influence in the Philharmonic Society there, telling me that they were both staying with him one weekend, and as the Sunday was very wet they spent the day playing concertos, alternating solo violin and piano accompanist, and whichever way round they were playing, neither ever had a note of music.

I first heard Kreisler play the Beethoven and the Brahms with Sir Henry Wood when I was fourteen. Both were unforgettable performances.

THE LONDON PHILHARMONIC ORCHESTRA

Sir Adrian gave numerous radio talks on the orchestra that
became his home for a glorious Indian summer after his
compulsory retirement (to which he always referred as 'the
sack') from the B.B.C. The following essay includes material
from broadcasts in 1951, 1953 and 1961.

It is difficult for anyone who has not seen it to believe the
extraordinary change which has come over British orchestral
life since 1930. There were then no permanent orchestras,
except in Bournemouth — even the famous Hallé was engaged for just one concert each week, and in London Sir
Henry Wood could only give a contract which included about
fifty concerts spread over the winter season, and two months
of Promenades in August and September. Besides this was the
London Symphony Orchestra, which made itself responsible
for twenty concerts or so through the winter, and whose
eminent personnel also usually engaged themselves for two
months of opera at Covent Garden in the summer.

The quality of all this was high, for British players have
always had a wonderful ability to sight-read — forced on them
by the minimum of rehearsal which circumstances used to
demand — but concert-goers became restive when the opportunities came for comparison of their national quality with a
succession of post-war visitors during the 'twenties — from
Amsterdam, Berlin and Vienna, and finally in 1928 when
Toscanini came with the New York Philharmonic Symphony.

It was then realised that, though London need not be
ashamed of her players, skill was not enough, and they must
be given adequate chances of rehearsing together, and really
studying their work.

The first response to this was given by the B.B.C., with its
spectacular rise in resources and authority. In October 1930 it
launched the B.B.C. Symphony Orchestra at Queen's Hall,
and exactly two years later, in 1932, Sir Thomas Beecham
conducted the first concert of the London Philharmonic
Orchestra. Although mainly the orchestra of Sir Thomas
Beecham, the Orchestra was immediately announced to be

permanently attached to other organisations, like the Royal
Philharmonic Society, the Royal Choral Society, and the
summer season at Covent Garden.

The virtuosity of its founder was naturally communicated
to every man in the Orchestra, and at the opening concert,
when they played the *Carnaval Romain* Overture of Berlioz and
Strauss' *Ein Heldenleben*, they achieved a most enviable
reputation.

Through the seven years of uncertain peace the Orchestra and its conductor adorned the London concert world, and,
besides, found time to tour the provinces periodically, and
also, in Germany, sought the approval of Hitler and his
lieutenants, as well as undertaking a considerable recording
programme.

The outbreak of war in 1939 was a severe blow to the
Orchestra; there were few who thought it would survive. They
reckoned without a rank and file member, Mr. Thomas
Russell, who with great spirit gathered the Orchestra
together, formed round him a loyal band of directors, and,
while concerts were still forbidden in bomb-fearing London,
put the instruments on any possible kind of transport, and
raided the municipal halls of any towns which would receive
them, accumulating any audience they could in the black-out,
going back by coach as often as possible to their families in
London for what was left of the night. Not unnaturally,
personalities in organisations change from time to time, and
whilst this has been the case in the London Philharmonic
Orchestra, the principle of government by its own players still
exists to-day.

I was often privileged to visit the L.P.O. through these
war years. I was asked to join the Orchestra in Blackburn on a
certain day in January, and, not knowing the town, I decided
to go up to Preston, where I knew the Renbury Hotel, and get
over the few miles to Blackburn as best I could in time for
rehearsal next morning. I was delighted to find a train for this,
but when I got to Blackburn I was made to feel rather
ashamed of my comfort-seeking arrangements, for the Orchestra, arriving at Blackburn about 11 p.m. after a concert in
Manchester, or somewhere, found they just couldn't cope with
the snow and the blackout, and so, rather than hunting for

digs under these difficulties, nearly all of them had slept in the station waiting-rooms. They were all there at ten for rehearsal and everything went according to plan, in spite of their discomfort. I remember in those days one of the most popular towns visited by the L.P.O. was Cheltenham. The concert hall is also the spa building and the spacious corridors are well provided with most comfortable sofas — no one bothered about digs on these nights.

On another occasion, during rehearsal, I was told that the programmes had not arrived from London, and so I had to introduce each item to the audience as we went along. One night after a concert, most of the players left their instruments in Queen's Hall as they had a rehearsal and concert there next day. That was the very night when Queen's Hall was bombed. The hall was in ruins and the instruments lost, but as a result of an appeal instruments poured in from all over the country.

As the war went on, it was possible to organise better, and plan further ahead. Some most successful concerts took place in variety theatres in larger cities, and the Orchestra also was able to form itself into a limited company with its members as shareholders, and a board of directors, elected by the players from their own membership. This is how the Orchestra is now governed and its machinery seems ready to stand up successfully to any strain or emergency.

There are, as you know, very few orchestras in the world which do not work to one or more permanent conductors. These rare few throw a pretty big responsibility on to their directors, for the artistic development of an orchestra seems essentially to need the control of a single mind. The London Philharmonic Orchestra did, in effect, carry on in this way all through the war, and war conditions, calling as they did more for improvisation than for a long-term view, suited the policy reasonably well.

After the war was over, a long list of world-famous musicians were invited as guest conductors — Bruno Walter, Furtwangler, de Sabata, Kleiber, Ansermet, and a host of others — a move which did much to re-establish international standards in London's concert life. There were one or two others as well whose names were not so familiar then as they are today, and who owe much to the Orchestra's perspicacity in recognising their promise and giving them their opportunity in no half-hearted fashion.

But although this policy led to a series of individually brilliant and exciting concerts, it did not afford the long-term training under a single man which a permanent orchestra needs if it is going to develop a style of its own. So the Directors were still on the lookout and in 1949 persuaded Edward van Beinum to come to them, without giving up his work in Holland, for two- and three-month periods as often as it could be arranged.

But Mr. van Beinum found it increasingly difficult to spare so much time for London, as he was also in demand in America and elsewhere, and so, when I had to leave the B.B.C., under their too-old-at-sixty rule, I was very pleased to get an invitation from the London Philharmonic Orchestra.

It has been hard work — few people realise how hard the L.P.O. does work. A typical week may well include six evening concerts in places as widely separated as Folkestone, Watford, Herne Bay, Southampton and Brighton, if there is no London concert. Four or five of these mornings may well be spent rehearsing, or perhaps giving children's concerts somewhere in outer London, with the journey down to the country by coach in the afternoon, and return to London after the concert. It is usually a relief — particularly in winter — when one or two London concerts, or two or three days' recording in London, come into any week, for then we can see a little more of our homes and families. I say 'we', but you can well imagine that an elderly conductor can't possibly keep up the pace I have described, and turn up night after night with the Orchestra at these far-flung centres. I nearly kept up with it for a few months at first, but I soon had to give in, and I now am detailed only for considerably less than half the concerts at which the Orchestra plays. I am not by nature a guest conductor; I like to go on and on working with the same people and trying to develop and mature the performances all the time. As someone once said to me, 'In rehearsal you like to say fresh things to the same people rather than the same thing to fresh people'.

The Orchestra has been abroad on a number of occasions; in 1951 we had a strenuous German tour (I think it was thirteen concerts in thirteen days, including Berlin, Hamburg, the Ruhr, Munich, Nürnberg and Heidelberg). Not content with that, we recrossed by the night boat to Harwich, and played in Ipswich that afternoon. There are very vivid impressions of those days; in Münster (Westphalia), an enormous place like Olympia which was packed tight with an audience many of whom had come long distances. The beautiful little Opera House at Nürnberg, and the visit to my room after the concert of a great-niece of Schumann's — we had just played the Fourth Symphony — and the only disappointment, Düsseldorf, where a large cinema-like hall was only half full because the English Welfare Officer had forgotten to make plans for the British troops and their families to buy tickets in German currency. I'm afraid I still have the schoolboy's excitement about travel gadgets, and for this tour the German Railways had given us a little special train with our own dining-car and sleepers, when necessary, so that we were always more than adequately cared for. We sometimes think of that special train when we have to make a winter journey by road after a concert in Folkestone or Southampton because there just isn't a train.

In 1956 we were invited to visit the U.S.S.R., the first British Orchestra to do so, where we were welcomed with tremendous enthusiasm for nine concerts in Moscow and Leningrad. We played programmes of nearly 50 per cent British music (at their own request) to packed houses nightly for three weeks, and followed this with a long German tour and three days in Paris. Again one thinks of very long railway journeys (though the trains, particularly the night trains between Leningrad and Moscow, are very finely equipped) and some wonderful sights: a sunset seen over the golden domes of the Kremlin; the gay colours of St. Basil's Cathedral; the Red Square; Peterhof, its frontiers and its view across the sea to Finland; the magnificent lay-out of the centre of Leningrad with the Winter Palace, the Admiralty and the Hermitage Gallery all looking over the superb sweep of the Neva — these are permanent memories of an exciting month. A number of English works were performed to Russian audiences for the first time, including two of Vaughan Williams' Symphonies, Nos. 4 and 5, *The Planets* of Holst, the 'Four Sea

Interludes' from *Peter Grimes* by Benjamin Britten, and Walton's First Symphony.

Apart from its main concert activities the L.P.O. has
made many important recordings since the war in addition to
the great number made under Sir Thomas Beecham and guest
conductors before the war. One of the highlights of this side of
their work was the recording of the first eight Vaughan
Williams Symphonies in the presence of the composer, then,
subsequently, the Ninth, and on the morning the recording
was scheduled to start the composer died. Of this association
with one of the greatest composers of our age, both the
Orchestra and I myself have felt extremely proud.

The L.P.O. has encouraged the young English conductor
for a number of years, giving regular opportunities for audi-
tion rehearsals or part of a normal concert programme.

Since 1945 the L.P.O. has invited many of the leading
conductors of the world to spend periods working with it, both
in London and provincial towns, and since 1959 its London
programme has been presented by the newly-formed London
Philharmonic Society, whose enterprising planning and presentation have earned praise from all quarters.

The management of the L.P.O. maintains a very full
schedule of work each year, but is looking forward to the time
when sufficient subsidies are available to enable them to offer
the musicians some form of security as opposed to the present
free-lance method of engagement, and to enable them to
devote ample rehearsal time to all their needs.

YEHUDI MENUHIN

Sir Adrian presented the Gold Medal of the Royal Philharmonic Society to Yehudi Menuhin on 7 November 1962. This is
the text of his address.

I count it a great honour to have been asked by the Directors
of the Royal Philharmonic Society to give their coveted Gold
Medal to Mr. Yehudi Menuhin — a task to which someone of

Cabinet rank could be expected to find appropriate words for such an exceptionally notable occasion.

I expect that many of you will have seen the very impressive list of Gold Medallists in the brochure which the Society has published for its 150th birthday, and you will know that the Medal was first struck nearly a century ago, and has been awarded to about sixty of the leading musicians of the period. You may not have noticed that the list includes only four violinists — Joseph Joachim, Eugène Ysaÿe, Fritz Kreisler and Jan Kubelík. I am old enough to have heard them all, and I can tell you that tonight's performance will take its place in my memory with the achievements of those four giants of former days.

There is a special quality of our medallist's playing which is not noticed as often as it might be, I think. You have the magnificent physique of a man in his middle forties, and a splendidly youthful energy. But he began his career so early in life that there is also an artistic maturity that belongs to a man nearly twenty years older. His collaborator tonight, Maître Monteux, whom we are always thrilled to hear on this platform, combines a like maturity with what we can only describe as perennial youth!

When Mr. Paderewski (also a Gold Medallist, by the way) was last in London, one of our critical friends made this striking comment: 'Mr. Paderewski is a very good pianist, but there is something else: he is the greatest man who can play the piano to us'.

I feel that this applies in the same way to Mr. Menuhin. He has made himself a master in so many fields of thought and knowledge that he could have been a great man in many other ways, and if anyone had ever done such a disservice to music as to invite him to become prime minister of a great country, his achievement would, I am sure, be comparable to Mr. Paderewski's.

This Medal has always been awarded only after the most anxious thought and discussion, and always from an international point of view. Great foreign artists on the list considerably out-number the Britisher, and so it is always pleasant when a Britisher is considered to be worthy of this great honour. Mr. Menuhin is an American citizen, but I want to

claim him as almost a fellow-countryman. He has a charming
British wife and a home in this country; he stays and works
here for long periods; and his sons are at school here.

And so it gives me very great pleasure to hand this Medal
to Mr. Menuhin. I give it with the gratitude of the Royal
Philharmonic Society's Directors; with the gratitude of this
great audience; with the gratitude of countless other admirers
who are not with us tonight; and with that kind of gratitude
which doesn't think only of the past, but can also look forward
to a long future of equally splendid performances.

GLENN MILLER

Sir Adrian contributed this reminiscence to a radio
programme in 1953.

As conductor of the B.B.C. Symphony Orchestra when our
war headquarters were at Bedford, I saw quite a lot of the
Miller band. I often dropped in on their rehearsals, since they
used the Corn Exchange, as we did. I found it fascinating to
watch Glenn Miller at work. He was a thorough craftsman: he
knew just what he wanted to get from his band and how to get
it, and he didn't mind how hard he worked himself or them.

Of course, it was the string section which interested me
most — twenty players, all from famous orchestras (there
were actually some who had played under me in America). I
always enjoyed their programme, 'Strings with Wings',
although I wished they could have been playing better stuff.

Glenn Miller liked seeing me at his rehearsals, I think,
and one day asked me if I'd like to conduct 'Strings with
Wings' myself. I was delighted to, and I still remember that
little programme we did in November, 1944, although it was
only fifteen minutes long. We played, amongst other things,
an arrangement for strings of the beautiful 'Cloud' Nocturne
of Debussy. It was arranged by a member of the band, Mr.
George Ockner, who very kindly gave me a copy of his
arrangement. Some idea of the friendliness and permanence of

these strings can be derived from the fact that when the writing was sub-divided to any considerable extent, leaving some soloists each playing a particular line, their names are inserted in the score — George, Harry, Ernie and Gene in the violins; Dave and Stan on the viola line were the most prominent.

I hope I may have the pleasure of seeing some of them again if I go to the United States. We certainly missed them when they left Bedford.

ALBERT SAMMONS

Albert Sammons died in August 1957. In November of that year Sir Adrian broadcast this tribute to him on the B.B.C.'s Home Service.

For a number of reasons, Albert Sammons takes a very special place in the history of British music-making. He leapt into fame soon after the 1914 war began by playing the Elgar Concerto, which had hitherto pretty well been Kreisler's monopoly, and by playing it in a way that everybody, including the composer, felt was as essentially right as Kreisler's even though it differed considerably.

He undertook this performance when he was following the career of an orchestral player, and he had had no special preparations, no training abroad, no scholarship luxuries such as are at the disposal of gifted youngsters nowadays. And so his career went on from there on simple, uneventful, English lines. He refused many invitations to play abroad — the career of international celebrity did not interest him — but by his sterling integrity and lovely mastery of his instrument he became instantly the leader of the British violin world, and remained in this position all his life.

Sammons was no specialist; he loved all kinds of music, and, say, the rather rarified idiom of Gabriel Fauré was well within his grasp. Fauré's lovely songs are perhaps his greatest contribution to music, but he wrote a good deal of beautiful

chamber music, and Sammons understood this sympatheti-
cally, for he was a player not only of concertos and music on
the grand scale — he unbent most graciously.

The records he made can give you no idea of his splendid
personal qualities, of the devotion of his pupils, and fellow
artists, and his selfless interest in music-making of all kinds,
whether in Queen's Hall or some humble mission room
perhaps in far-off Wales or Scotland. He was a great musician
in every sense of the word.

PART FIVE

ON MUSIC
IN GENERAL

———————————•————————————

MUSIC AND POLITICS

Sir Adrian wrote this essay for the magazine *European Affairs* in October 1949.

A distinguished American lawyer recently said to me that a fine performance of a Beethoven Symphony could move him far more deeply than any kind of preaching. Although that may not be everybody's experience (much as I wish that it were, I rather fancy that it is not), I feel that there is a good deal in the belief that the spiritual power of great music can sometimes go beyond the meaning of words. And I have often wondered how music can be best used to heal some of the wounds of a divided world by that very spiritual power. (My eminent colleague Dr. Koussevitzky no doubt had similar feelings about this matter, for not so very long ago he submitted that it would be a good idea if all members of international conferences were forced to listen to a symphony concert or opera for a couple of hours every evening! Perhaps, however, this might be seen as a form of 'punishment' or 'medicine' to be inflicted on such statesmen.)

Seriously speaking, I do think that music opens up immense spiritual and psychological resources in the task of lessening some of the misunderstandings which result in political conflicts and their attendant social disasters.

Once when I was Director of Music to the British

Broadcasting Corporation, a distinguished ex-soldier who had taken over control of the programme output of the B.B.C., said to me: 'I left the Army and came to the B.B.C., simply because I felt that if anything can prevent another war, broadcasting will do it. This I feel to be the first duty of broadcasting. Now, how are your crotchets and quavers going to help us to stop war?'

That question has haunted me ever since. And now I am more convinced than ever that interpreters of the great tone-poets also have some duty in working for that kind of understanding and spiritual harmony, without which civilisation cannot go forward.

How, indeed, can the language of music help? Being abstract and universal, this language is already a unifying force among the peoples of the world. The interpretative powers of executants, and the guidance and clarification which musicologists and historians are able to offer, seem to be sufficient in spreading its message. Nevertheless, there is something which nations and organisations can do to enhance its function, especially in these times of conflicting ideologies and power politics.

I feel that there is insufficient *personal* contact between musicians, whether singers, pianists, conductors or composers. Not even composers, given as they are to battling with creative problems in a seemingly abstract world of sound, can afford to do without that kind of liaison. Understanding will always remain a powerful weapon in solving complicated world problems, and governments must learn to depend more on art in gathering together the threads of such understanding. They would do well, therefore, if they systematically subsidised the visits of certain orchestras and composers to other countries.

From my own experience I have learnt to appreciate the usefulness of personal contact. During my work for the British Council I have always felt that personal contacts with fellow musicians in other countries have not only confirmed but actually widened the universality of music in its power to transcend frontiers and misunderstanding. There was a strong feeling that something really concrete had been achieved when, for instance, the B.B.C. Symphony Orchestra was allowed to entertain the Berlin and Vienna Philharmonic Orchestras. When will we be able to welcome someone like Dmitri Shostakovich to this country and when will someone like our own Benjamin Britten be able to return such a compliment in Soviet Russia?

All misunderstandings, political ones included, are evil in essence. We need the help of the language of music to make them less formidable.

CONCENTRATION AND PERFORMANCE

This is the address Sir Adrian gave in September 1950 to the Conference of the National Federation of Music Societies.

I sometimes try to think down to the fundamentals governing our lives as musicians (whether amateur or professional) and the terrific attraction that holds us to the art, and enthrals and revivifies even those of us who are most overworked. It is the same thing that one can see in the faces of all the young people who occupy the Promenade at the Henry Wood Concerts — that concentration which makes them forget that they are standing to listen to over two hours' music, and perhaps have been standing in the queue outside before that. It is a force that kept people going to concerts even when bombs were dropping, and it ties to the profession men who might well go to easier jobs, and thereby perhaps even increase their incomes.

I once heard our great contemporary, Ralph Vaughan Williams, talking to the members of the village choirs at a festival held in the depths of a country district in the south, and describing to them how the ordinary healthy Englishman now and then gets an urge inside him which sends him, when possible, out of doors either to kill something or to push a ball about somehow. This urge, he said, affects some people differently, for when they get the urge, instead of going out of doors with a ball or a fishing-rod they go to their writing-tables, and there scatter dots and dashes all over some curiously ruled paper. This happy parallel was then brought straight home to us, and we were told that whenever we take up a copy of those queer dots and dashes, with the intention of converting them into sound, our duty includes not only the accurate and faithful performance of that music, but also with it the conveyance of that urge which would send the normal Englishman out of doors with a ball.

This, of course, means a strong effort of concentration on the part of everyone concerned. Concentration is a power we all possess, but it can be enormously developed if we put our minds to it. It is an essential part of the work of any artist, writer or speaker, and in our own sphere I can quote some remarkable examples.

At Toscanini's very first rehearsal in London, he began with the Brahms E minor. It went well, so well that he played through the slow movement without stopping, and only gathered up a few points in it afterwards. I noticed that a number of things, at that first run-through, had been different from the usual practice of the orchestra, which of course often played that Symphony with me. Subtle points of dynamics, shading and phrasing were played appreciably different from usual. I asked some of the players afterwards whether they knew why they were playing them differently. 'No,' they said, 'but we were quite certain that was how he wanted it.' I have heard of Weingartner playing a work through twice or three times hardly saying a word, and the players knew each time they were playing more and more as he wanted it.

Another story concerns concentration of a different kind. Many years ago I was asked to go and help at a boys' preparatory school. It finished with a group of folksongs sung by the whole school, packed on the platform. They gave an electric performance, and after it was over I congratulated Armstrong Gibbs — for it was he who was in charge — and asked him how he did it. 'Well,' was the reply, 'I make each boy personally responsible that his parents know exactly what the folksongs are all about.' And so we not only felt and understood these folksongs as never before, but we could see each little boy's eyes fixed on his parents, as if defying them and all of us to miss a single word of those songs.

There is an example of how everyone — professionals included — can sometimes learn in unexpected places. I know well that many of my deepest and most moving experiences in music have come at times when I have been associated with amateurs (in most cases, grown-up). The real essence of music — that greatness that lies beneath and behind the sound that music makes — is often clearer to them than to the workaday practitioner whose life is devoted to the job, and who knows so much of music that some of it can easily lose its full intensity at times.

Those little boys taught me something else as well as their intense concentration. There was all the best of the amateur, but Armstrong Gibbs' teaching had given them also what I feel to be the last thing the amateur (particularly the amateur soloist) learns, the absence of which is, usually, the ultimate distinction between amateur and professional, though it is also a difficult enough thing for a young professional to learn. Dame Myra Hess has said that no one can give a good recital who cannot also give a good party, and, listening to music, we can all of us recall occasions when the performance has been beautiful in many ways, but has not managed to grip us because the performer seems somehow to have been playing (or singing) to himself, and has failed to convey, to project, the essence and the meaning of his music to us. He has not somehow made us properly welcome at his party, and hasn't really included us in the circle of his friends, ready to share everything with us as a good host should. Dr. Gibbs told me that if any of his boys happened to have no parents at the concert, he made them fix on someone in the back row, imagine that person was a little deaf, and then take the responsibility for his enjoyment and understanding of the folksong.

And so we were caught up by our hosts, we were included in the party, and it would indeed have been difficult for us to have thought about something else if we had tried. I can remember how Paderewski in a couple of bars brought one face to face with Beethoven or Chopin, or whoever it might be, and one's thought was chained, and concentration no effort.

There is one other factor in this matter of projection that I would like to think about for a moment. I can remember feeling, as a boy of fifteen, when it was my privilege to attend many splendid concerts, that the symphony, or whatever it was, when the performance was over, became something solid and static; it stood there before me like the North Front of Westminster Abbey, past which I walked every day at that time. I wrote home of one performance, and said that it seemed as if the four movements were written out on two great pages, and the whole score was before me at one glance. Hans Richter, Wagner's friend and helper in so many ways, had this quality to such an extent that when his all-commanding stick came down on that first low E flat at the opening of *Das Rheingold*, one felt that only an earthquake could prevent our being swept on and on to that final D flat major of *Götterdämmerung* four evenings later.

What is the secret of this inexorable sweep of the greatest performances? It is hard to say, but I can tell you one thing that will easily prevent it, and that is over-attention to detail. The pianist who sticks for hours, practising page one before he has looked at the rest of the sonata; the singer who works at his technique in the first verse before he has really absorbed the poem; and, worst of all, the conductor who starts practising bar 13 with his violas before they have any idea how the overture is going to finish; all these are stifling at birth the real breath of the music, and making it impossible to recapture that bird's eye view of the piece as a whole which must always be in the mind of the great performer, however much he has to practise details later on *after* he has absorbed the general picture.

In academic circles structure and balance form perhaps the most important part of the study of a musical work; but are we performers always as conscious as we should be of its paramount importance to our playing and singing? Can we, at a moment's notice, call to mind the shape of any work we love; its sequence of keys; its emotional rise and fall; its dynamic high spots? Without it, can we confidently feel that we have fully equipped ourselves for our performance; can we really undertake the responsibility of conveying the mighty thoughts of a Bach or a Beethoven to eager listeners who have trusted themselves to our guidance? It is a great responsibility we carry, and no amount of care in preparation can ever be too much if we are going to be true to our task, and bring the music we live for to those who have had fewer opportunities, and so further the work our Federation is so splendidly equipped to help on, by spreading the flame far and wide and bringing the glorious message of great music to a larger and larger audience every year.

CONCENTRATION AND LISTENING

This essay was written 'for Hubert Foss' of Oxford University Press in December 1946, although not published by O.U.P.

How long are you able to concentrate on listening to music? I ask this question because recently in an unguarded moment I let slip the opinion that the Promenade Concerts were far too long, and this called down upon my head the wrath of a number of insatiable young Promenaders, who insisted that they were quite happy to endure a nightly dose of two and a half hours of symphonic music and even to stand up to it. Well, I don't believe I have ever *really listened* to music for more than an hour and a half on end, and if I am sitting through a concert that is longer than this I consciously take it easy during at least one piece in order that I may be fresh enough to listen to what I may consider more important. When I say 'take it easy', I don't mean that I go to sleep (necessarily); I just let the stuff agreeably trickle in at one ear, and it is quite probable that most of it disappears at once out of the other.

All this reminds me of an amusing experience soon after the last war, when as an eager young professional, I had gone to Munich with some friends to wallow in opera at the Festival. I ran into Dame Ethel Smyth one evening and she horrified me by saying, 'I've invited Bruno Walter and his family to dine with me during this awful Second Act of *Die Walküre*' — she was a most imperfect Wagnerite — 'and you must join us'. Well, I was a conscientious festival-goer, I am also gifted with a 25 per cent allowance of Scottish blood, and I very nearly resisted the monstrous proposal, but the bait of seeing more of Bruno Walter (whom I had then only just met) was too tempting, and we had a most cheery and fascinating party, and could feel a wonderful superiority (even if tinged with envy) over the crowds who poured out after the Second Act and began scrambling for their beer, salad and sandwiches.

Now the point of all this is that as the Third Act unrolled itself to my astonished attention, I realised that I was listening to it as if for the first time. I thought I had heard *The Ring* eight or ten times already — I had borrowed vocal scores and played through most of them a good deal — I had often heard even the less hackneyed of the 'bleeding chunks' which in those days far more than now found their way into most orchestral programmes, but here was the dear old Third Act of *Walküre* penetrating where it had never reached before. After this I always took my Wagner in doses of two acts at a time, and the Munich experience was repeated in the Third Acts every time.

Perhaps I am a slower listener than most people — perhaps I concentrate more deeply, though I can hardly believe this when I sit (on an off-night) and watch the faces of the Promenaders: *there* is concentration, if anywhere, and I simply don't understand how they can keep it up night after night for two months.

One thing I know: the performers are unanimously in favour of a reduction to two hours or less; but that is another story!

SOUND AND SPACE

This short talk was broadcast in May 1960.

Hans Richter retired from his winter job with the Hallé Orchestra, and his summer job doing the German operas at Covent Garden, just about fifty years ago. I remember soon after this that I was talking to a very observant and sensitive musician, and I was struck by a remark he made: 'You remember the plan of all the Old Man's programmes' (this was the affectionate nickname he had in the London orchestral world). 'A good deal of noise to start with — Wagner, Tchaikovsky, Strauss — until the interval, when half the orchestra packed up and went home, and the other half stayed and played a Haydn, Mozart or Beethoven symphony. Did you ever notice that the half who stayed behind made twice as much sound as the full orchestra that had been there at first?'

In these days I suppose it would be possible to measure the decibels and tell us whether this was an illusion, or really true. I certainly felt that it was true. My friend's main reason was that Strauss and Wagner with at least ten brass instruments had their chording laid on too thickly, while the resonance and brilliance of Mozart's two horns and two trumpets, spaced at an octave's or at any rate a sixth's distance from each other, just fitted the Queen's Hall acoustics and rang through the place freely and openly.

I was thinking of all this a short time ago as I listened in Westminster Abbey to the glorious tone of Yehudi Menuhin's violin playing Bach. The congregation was silent and spellbound, and there wasn't a cough at all through the eighty minutes of music. So the single instrument seemed to fill the whole of that great building as completely as the Coronation choir and orchestra had done seven years ago, and in particular the tremendous chording in the *Chaconne*, perfectly tuned and spaced, rang out surely as never before. Mr. Menuhin stood on a raised platform right under the lantern, so that the tone could rise easily to the roof and run along it in every direction. I wish I could have heard some of it from the nave. I am told that it seemed distant there, but was still wonderfully clear. Mr. Menuhin's intonation was flawless, so in this way, too, he gained maximum resonance.

Whenever I am able to reach the top gallery of the Royal Albert Hall, I always feel it is an ideal place to listen from. The sound is clear and the quality somehow purified, and the balance far better than anywhere else in the Hall. It isn't at all necessary to sit in front; in fact I prefer the back: like the people in the nave at Westminster you can see nothing, and as there are not many chairs you find people lying on the floor drinking in the sound in a dedicated and impersonal atmosphere. It is the music that matters up there, not the performer. So there are, I think, occasions when distance lends enchantment, and space, in two senses of the term, is a help to the ideal projection of fine music.

WHO IS THE ORCHESTRA?

In 1942 the B.B.C. Forces Programme ran a series entitled 'The Orchestra Speaks', in which members of the B.B.C. Symphony Orchestra talked about themselves and their approach to their art. Sir Adrian contributed the last programme in the series.

The performance of music is such an intangible thing that strangers are, I think, a bit apt to misjudge its daily round and think that all we do (conductors included) is to have a good time all day and then trot round to the studio in the evening, get our instruments and music out, and play away. It is easy to forget that a player in a symphony orchestra has probably begun to learn his instrument as a child, has devoted several years to an intensive study of its technique, as well as other aspects of music — history, orchestration, form — has probably learnt several other instruments into the bargain, and then before seeking a post in a symphony orchestra has spent several years accumulating experience in an organisation that is less auspicious, but where perhaps individual responsibility is greater. Nearly every day all his life, he probably devotes some time to practice, and many of my orchestral friends often show me how up-to-date they are in their reading of current musical books as well as general literature. Again, players will often take their own parts home to study, especially in a new work. Only this week a violinist told me that he had spent three hours trying and practising a long passage in a new work which had (to put it mildly) not been written with any great regard to the technical possibilities of the violin!

Now, I don't think the individuals who have contributed to 'The Orchestra Speaks' have told you much about their hobbies. There is quite a staggering range of these. In the B.B.C. we have over forty people who understand the game of chess; gardeners and photographers are legion; two are efficient watch repairers, and one has actually made himself a beautiful little watch which sits in his button-hole. Needless to say, his skill has now (worse luck for us) been transferred to the workshops of the R.A.F. Travellers, too, are legion, and good stories are exchanged at the end of the summer holidays, but I don't think we can compete with our friend in the London Philharmonic Orchestra who hiked over the Caucasus!

So much for the individual. As a corporate unit, the orchestra has to work itself in by a never-ending chain of rehearsals. The keen artist is never satisfied, and even if only a few days elapse between two performances of the same work, I find I can usually manage to spend twenty minutes or so trying to ensure that the second performance is in some way an improvement on the first. It is very sad that war difficulties are now forcing some orchestras to reduce their rehearsals quite drastically, but it is an evidence of great skill and musicianship that their performances under these conditions are still very fine. With ordinary repertoire programmes, we usually allow time in the B.B.C. for a rehearsal three times as long as the performance, that is, with a programme lasting an hour, we allow a three-hour rehearsal.

You can imagine what a privilege it is to be the conductor of an organisation which brings together such a group of personalities, and you can perhaps see a little how much the conductor depends on his players. I think it is true to say that the further an orchestra goes in skill, in maturity and expressive range, the more the conductor leaves to the leaders. Before we left London, when we were enlarging our repertoire much faster than we do now, every new work of any importance was preceded by separate rehearsals for wind and strings, and part of the string rehearsal was subdivided into each group, working with its own leader, while I toured round from room to room in case any points arose that wanted my help. The leaders had already written their suggestions for fingering and bowing on the parts, and these were now put to the test. I should like to say how lucky I feel myself in having almost daily worked with such a magnificent body of players as the B.B.C. Orchestra.

MUSIC OF THE WEEK

The next two talks are examples of the regular broadcasts on 'Music of the Week' Sir Adrian gave when the B.B.C.'s Director of Music.

I. Welcome to Casals

This talk was broadcast on 14 November 1937.

Maestro Toscanini left us characteristically by air at seven in the morning after his last concert, still lyrical, even at that early hour, in his praise of the choir and orchestra which, I think you will agree, did rise superbly to his demands. Now we look forward to the visit of another giant whose principal work has been in another field of music. I mean, of course, Pau Casals, a master of the violoncello, who has reigned supreme both in Europe and America for more than thirty years. I can remember when he first came, how all the 'cellists in London used to flock to his recitals, filled with amazement at what was considered at that time the unorthodox nature of his technique. We needn't go into all that now, but one of his peculiarities consists in having a thick piece of cork on his bow where he holds it. This seems to me a most sensible arrangement, as a bow is a very slim thing to hold for any length of time. Many conductors like a cork handle to their sticks for the same reason, and I personally find I am apt to get cramp if I try to hold a very thin piece of plain wood with nothing round it. My hand is on the large side, but I think cork is always a good thing.

But whatever his method he amazed us most of all I think by his power to infuse such beauty, variety and completeness into the unaccompanied Suites of Bach which up to that time had been very much neglected. With the exception of Paderewski, Casals is, I think, the only artist in Europe who is recognised as a great man by those who are not interested in his music. One of the principal avenues in Barcelona is called after him, and recently in the revolution when the Church in Vendrell, where his father was organist and where he had played as a boy, was threatened by a destructive mob, another crowd turned up to protect it. After a fight the precious organ was saved as a mark of respect to Casals, which touched him very much indeed.

I first met Dr. Casals (I say 'Doctor' because I am proud to claim him as a colleague: we are both honorary Doctors of Music of the University of Edinburgh) in Liverpool soon after the War, when I had the great experience of conducting the Schumann 'Cello Concerto for him.

I have suggested that Dr. Casals is recognised as one of the biggest men in Catalonia. He had also a great influence on broadcasting, and hopes through this, coupled with the work of his orchestra, to build up the music of Catalonia to a height worthy of its great folksong traditions. The collapse of it all in the revolution has been a great blow to him, and we may all sympathise and wish that when the new Spain arises there may be found scope and opportunity for a quick rebirth of all his plans.

One of the delightful things about music is that, itself a language, it fosters international friendships between great musicians who otherwise would perhaps be kept apart by the bar of language, and the rareness of their opportunities for meeting. Strauss and Elgar were a well-known example, and the affection and respect between Sibelius and Bantock are also well-known. Casals is happily a frequent visitor to England and talks excellent English, but even without this he would, I think, claim Sir Donald Tovey as a great friend.

Trained in music from a very early age, Donald Tovey was already recognised by men of the stamp of Joachim and Richter as being one of the most musical musicians in Europe, as well has having a memory which could only be called staggering. His penetration into the mind of a composer is quite extraordinary, as shown by his work on Bach's *Art of Fugue* — in fact, by all his critical and analytical writings. I find these more and more stimulating and inspiring as I reread them parallel to my study of the great scores. I spoke a week or two ago of his fine work with the Reid Orchestra from time to time, but I didn't then speak of him as a composer. He has written much fine music, of which Dr. Colles has happily said: 'His mind, steeped in the classics and superior to popular demand, has produced works which musicians respect but the public is apt to ignore to its own loss'.

The latest of these works is the Concerto for Violoncello, written in honour of Casals by his friend, Donald Francis Tovey, as the title-page says. It takes about an hour to play. In these days of rapid thinking, it is right that we should be properly prepared when we have to face up to a really big canvas, superbly proportioned though it be, for unless we grasp its size at the outset we may get confused and its splendid plan be lost to us. The full score has been published in facsimile of the composer's own writing and has some very interesting devices in notation which his experience as a conductor has no doubt dictated. I find these reproductions of the composer's manuscript extraordinarily eloquent and helpful somehow or other, much more so than the printed page. It may interest you to hear that when I was studying the Mozart E flat Symphony for our concert last Wednesday, I was so baffled by the discrepancies between the different set editions of that work that I have that I am trying now to send to Germany to get the manuscript (which is in Berlin) photographed so that we shall be able next time to do it for you to give you something really approximating to Mozart's own phrasing.

To come back to the Tovey Concerto, there are four movements, of which the first lasts thirty minutes, and is a splendid structure in the great classical concerto form. In the words of the composer, the violoncello stands out for the most part as a restraining and calming influence against the tragic and stormy background. This is the basis of the movement. Then comes the lovely slow movement, followed by a tiny and very graceful intermezzo. The finale, the fourth movement, again shows a play on contrasted temperaments between the soloist and orchestra, this time in a considerably lighter vein. There is even some gentle leg-pulling as the argument pro-

ceeds, and the finish is decidedly unconventional. I am glad to
say Sir Donald hopes to be with us at the performance next
Wednesday. Dr. Casals then puts aside his 'cello and takes
charge of our orchestra in a very interesting programme,
including a Schubert Symphony a week today. But that
should properly belong to my next talk.

II. Choosing New Music

This talk discussed 'Music of the Week' following Sunday,
27 February 1938.

February is our usual month for the examination of new
music, and it occurs to me that you might like to hear
something about how this is done. Next week, too, I should
like to tell you a little about the working and management of
our B.B.C. Music Department.

I do not think I have ever told you about the three
outside advisers, well-known professional musicians who
come weekly to Broadcasting House and go through our
music programmes with us, criticising, commenting and
making valuable constructive suggestions. Besides their work
at this meeting we make use of their services as outside
assessors for the reading of scores in conjunction with other
members of our own staff.

I have said that February is the month when we invite
manuscripts to be sent us, and though a small number come
uninvited at other times of the year or demand special
treatment for some reason, we find it much better to collect
them once a year like this, as the readers can concentrate more
closely on the work and there is still more certainty of their
keeping uniform standard. There is then time for us to digest
the reports and the works that are chosen can go into the
following winter's programme. I need hardly say that the
great proportion of work examined in this way is by British
composers. Last year 210 scores reached us and were reported
on and examined by four or five assessors.

These reports have to be considered also in the light of
the most suitable place in programmes for the work in

question. As you probably know, the most striking and
advanced works find their way into the Contemporary series,
which occurs once a month on Fridays during the winter
before an invited audience at Broadcasting House. But there
will always be a large number of new works which by reason,
shall we say, of their less extreme style will be better placed in
general week-day programmes. A new work that is first heard
either at a Contemporary concert or in a week-day studio
programme will, if successful, pass on to a Promenade or a
Sunday Symphony concert. A recent example of this is
Howard Ferguson's *Partita* which we gave its second performance at our Sunday concert a week ago. I am also looking
forward to conducting it in Belfast next month.

Composers whose work is already well-known may find
their way straight into the Promenade or Sunday concerts, or
perhaps even Symphony concerts, but that is comparatively
rare. Music is, after all, to be heard and not to be seen; and it
is only when one has really heard an orchestral work that one
can begin to think of determining its true value and placing it
where it ought to be.

If I may be personal for a moment, I find that a good
many people I know are bewildered when I tell them that I
never read new scores myself. Surely this is a logical line to
take. I cannot possibly read them all, and surely it is best that
all should be in the hands of those who have the complete job
in hand and can judge fairly between the whole field of work
available. Besides, I think it is arguable that a man who
spends as much of his time as I do trying to make the finest
possible effect of the music that is put into his hands is not the
best person to criticise it. It is natural that as one studies work
for performance one sometimes notices weaknesses of con-
struction or orchestration or whatever it may be. It is surely
one's business not to dwell on those weaknesses more than is
necessary but to conceal them, and to throw the correspond-
ing good points in that work into prominence. That being so, I
cannot feel that an interpreter as such can be a good critic of
music.

I am sure that it is much wiser and fairer for me to have
the guidance of those who are experts at this particular thing
rather than to attempt to judge and possibly make unfair

decisions. I might also add that sometimes in summer we are able to arrange a few trial rehearsals at which we are enabled to hear some of the scores that have been submitted to us and better to form an opinion of them. You will remember that this has also formed an important part of the benevolent work of the Royal College of Music's Patrons' Fund, which was founded many years ago by Lord Palmer. I had the privilege of being the conductor of this Fund for a number of years, and it is a great delight to see the pleasure and to note the value of the experience which young composers — and sometimes experienced ones, too — derive from the chance of hearing their work rehearsed in this friendly, semi-private way before they were committed to the ordeal of public performance and of publication. Lord Palmer's beneficent foundation has done many splendid things for musicians, but none, I think, more useful than the work of these rehearsals.

I said that experienced composers, too, sometimes take advantage of this opportunity to hear their work in this way. And I remember our old friend, Gustav Holst, first conducting his first *Perfect Fool* ballet music at a Patrons' Fund rehearsal. I think I am right in saying that he was able to make a few small adjustments of scoring at that rehearsal which fortunately took place before the work was printed. This squares with the practice of Brahms, who never allowed a work to go to press until he had actually heard it.

The orchestral programmes just now are giving us some varied examples of the symphony. The Malipiero which you heard on Wednesday and can hear again in a couple of hours is, I think, a beautiful example of the terseness and economy that modern times have put back into the form. Its four movements total only twenty minutes, and it is so clearly the product of an alert Latin mind, keenly thoughtful and yet not without feeling. We have found Mr. Malipiero's neat, economical scoring to be as foolproof in its own way as Elgar's 'opulence and generosity'. Everything one sees on paper comes out clearly at the start of rehearsal. Another example is the Vaughan Williams F minor Symphony which Sir Henry Wood conducts on Wednesday — perhaps the most splendid of all his works: intensely vital, fierce in its clashes, full of the disturbed spirit of the modern world and yet in its slow

movement giving us a wonderful glimpse of serene and
natural beauty.

Then on Friday we have, not a symphony but a symphonic work, the Pianoforte Concerto of Alan Bush. Not yet forty,
Mr. Bush is a professor at the Royal Academy of Music,
where he' was a student. He was also a pupil of Dr. John
Ireland. A number of his works have already been broadcast,
notably a string quartet called *Dialectic* which has also been
given abroad. This Concerto is his most recent and most
important work. It is in four movements, the last of which is
written for baritone solo and male voice chorus, as well as the
pianoforte and orchestra. The composer's intention is to bring
his work into line with life and to link it up with some of the
problems of existence today, and the role of the chorus is to do
this by makig a direct appeal to the audience. Thus, their
opening words are: 'Friends, we would speak a little at this
performance'. The work ends with a forecast of the future and
a reference to a new world with giant Man, enormous in
freedom, rejoicing once more that all his powers are turned to
the goodness of all.

Another work by a living composer is Kodály's *Psalmus
Hungaricus* which Mr. Woodgate conducts on Tuesday. It is a
thrilling setting of the Fifty-fifth Psalm where King David
laments the treachery of his friends and the anger of the Lord,
but finally sounds a note of praise. Kodály is one of the leaders
of Hungarian music today and the Psalm was specially
written in 1923 for a festival concert which was part of the
celebration of the fiftieth anniversary of the union of Buda and
Pest as one city. He conducted the performance of the work
ten years ago at the Albert Hall for us and also at Gloucester
Festival.

Lovers of Debussy will be careful this week to make a
note of the five recitals of his songs in the Special Recitals
series. M. Pierre Bernac is coming over with M. Poulenc, the
distinguished composer, and we can look forward to exceptionally fine performances.

The programmes cover almost all the songs Debussy
wrote between 1880 and 1915, and include most of the
best-known groups.

Brass band lovers must not miss the Leicester Festival on

Saturday, and Sir Hugh Roberton's many admirers will rejoice to hear him and his Glasgow Orpheus Choir twice this week, on Tuesday and Saturday.

I want to add a word of apology about the Mozart *Serenade* for 13 wind instruments which we are playing at 6.30 this evening. The work lasts forty-eight minutes in its completeness, and that is how I would have wished to let you hear it, although it is a big strain on the players. Unfortunately, the few previous performances of the work of which we have records have been much cut, and so only thirty minutes have been allowed for it. By cutting the whole of the second movement and some repeats I hope we can give you a fairly true impression of this magnificent work, but I much hope that on some other occasion we can give it you absolutely complete.

SPEAKING FOR MYSELF

In 1949 Sir Adrian contributed a talk to the B.B.C.'s 'English Half-Hour' for the Far East, in which 'personalities from many walks of life' gave their views on a variety of subjects.

I wonder whether a man whose life is devoted to speaking for other people doesn't lose the power to speak for himself altogether. My work consists of absorbing as deeply and as thoroughly as possible the musical thoughts of composers as they have left them in cold print. I must then be ready to translate those thoughts into warm, living, throbbing sound; to give life to them so that they can spread their message to listeners of all types and ages. And what is that message? What is this mysterious sound that we call music? How is it that sound, when brought to order by the thoughts and feelings of the great men we call composers, and then brought to life by voices and instruments of all kinds, should have this profound effect on huge audiences?

There is no doubt about that effect. I am now at work conducting a fortnight of the famous Henry Wood Promenade

Concerts here in London. Every night we have the Albert Hall
full — seven thousand people or so, and twelve hundred of
them stand for two and a half hours listening to that music
after they have stood for perhaps an hour or more outside the
building waiting for admission. I love to go to those concerts
when I am not conducting, and can watch those young crowds
standing on the floor. There is a concentration in the expression of each one of them that shows that they have forgotten
whether they are standing or sitting. I took a non-musical
friend — a great airman — to a concert last season,and this is
what he wrote afterwards: 'I felt much impressed with the
Promenade Concert. I had no idea that serious music could
call up an atmosphere of such deep fellowship and concentration; a very slight twist would have made it one of devotion.'

Here then is a proof of my assertion that this mysterious
ordering of sound called music can have a profound effect on
most listeners; but the answer to my question 'why?' is more
difficult. It is obvious that music is the principal vehicle for
emotional expression; that is generally agreed, but why should
sound have this effect? We can only admit that though sight
may affect us deeply, sounds affects most of us more deeply.
(Smells, too, can call up powerful memories — perhaps some
day we shall have an art in scent!)

I am very sorry that I have never had the opportunity to
study the music of Asia, for I know that notably in India,
Pakistan, China and Japan a deeply sensitive and subtle art
has been developed over a far more extended period of
civilisation than our European mushroom growth of three or
four centuries; so much so that our Western ears have to be
specially trained to understand those subtleties of inflexion
and rhythm, while Eastern ears are able to apprehend our, in
some ways, cruder medium without much trouble — indeed,
European music is a special subject of study in some of the
countries I have mentioned. It may be that the extreme
refinement of oriental music has removed to a certain degree
the emotional impact. I don't know. But it is certain that
nowhere is music a greater stimulus to emotional activity than
in Africa, where it has developed least, and still retains its
more elementary rhythmic quality.

What then, is the place in life of this powerful emotional

language? I was much interested to hear Mr. E.M. Forster, in the opening talk of this series, maintaining that modern industrialism has ruined the 'glory of work' and the 'joy of work'. I think that this degeneration has affected us more in Europe than in the Far East, where craftsmanship has always held a most honoured place and, let us hope, will not be displaced by industrialism. Mr. Forster goes on to say: 'I am anxious that we should shake ourselves out of our conventional respect towards work, admit that it is a soul-scarifying nuisance, that leisure alone can have merit, and then be very careful how we spend our leisure'.

Yes, indeed: if prosperity comes again to Europe, it is greatly to be hoped that we shall learn to use our leisure more wisely than before. And here music must help. I have just come from America, where I conducted concerts in Toronto, New York and Chicago, and I have been amazed at the way in which this art of leisure has been developed during the twenty-five years since I first went there. The means of access to outdoor holidays, particularly for young people, have been enormously developed, and music has been linked with it in many ways and places. During my six weeks' tour I have seen no less than five outdoor concert series in action, and heard of many more. In most of these, arrangements are made so that the audience need not just come and listen to the music, but can picnic near by, and can take the music as part of a leisure afternoon or evening, incidental to it, but of paramount importance, for almost everywhere, once it began, there was complete silence and concentration on it.

One cannot talk of the good use of leisure without thinking how much we hurried Westerners can learn from the wisdom of the East in the matter of your command over time, and our subservience to it. I myself have become so much the slave of the clock that I always know what the time is (within a few minutes), and if my meal times are upset I am annoyed and probably get very bad-tempered. Curiously, I quite recently had a glimpse of that freedom from the fetters of time which the East understands so well. It was on my American trip, when I happened to have two or three days free in New York before my return sailing. It was very hot in the city and so I took a train out along Long Island, stopped at random at a seaside village, found a room almost by accident and then spent two days on an island off the coast, amongst sandhills, alone but for a few other bathers. There was a small restaurant there, but even the need for meals seemed less urgent, perhaps because American food is more nourishing than ours, and lasts longer, perhaps because the sun and the sea air were feeding me, too. But removed as I was from responsibility by three separate stages — first by the launch trip to the island, then by the railway from New York, and then by the Ocean from my working base — I seemed to get release from time in a way I had never known before.

I hope that this experience may not only help me in the future to get greater refreshment from my own leisure, but that it may give me greater strength to make my contribution, through music, to the leisure of my friends: the audience. To make audiences forget the passing of time while listening to music must surely be one of the goals of any performer.

INDEX

Adrian C Boult

STRAVINSKY SEEN AND HEARD
Hans Keller and Milein Cosman

In *Stravinsky Seen and Heard* Hans Keller and Milein Cosman concentrate on two different aspects of this multi-faceted composer.

Hans Keller analyses not only Stravinsky's conversion to serial technique but also those elements in his creative character, never yet touched upon, which made this dramatic change of mind possible.

Milein Cosman, who has long been known for her portrayal of musicians in action, contributes an extended series of over 60 drawings of Stravinsky at rehearsal, full of life and movement. Hans Keller's discoveries are thus complemented, throwing new light on one of the longest-established geniuses of our age, who yet remains a subject of controversy.

Stravinsky Seen and Heard also contains a full analysis of Stravinsky's serial technique, as used in his Dylan Thomas setting, 'Do not go gentle'.

'this marvellous . . . stimulating, valuable and utterly unique book . . . which anyone who professes to care about the state of twentieth century art should possess'

Music and Musicians

'stimulating'

Times Literary Supplement

'It's a brilliant and absorbing essay and the pictures are marvellous — got the old reptile superbly!'

Robert Simpson

128pp; index
£5.95 (hardcover)
£2.95 (softcover)

THE PROMS AND NATURAL JUSTICE
A Plan for Renewal
ROBERT SIMPSON
With a Foreword by
Sir Adrian Boult

In this important and provocative book Robert Simpson, for nearly thirty years a BBC Music Producer, scrutinises the methods by which the Proms are planned.

At present, the BBC allows the Controller, Music the absolute right to decide Prom programmes until death or retirement. Basing his reasoning on long experience inside the BBC, Dr Simpson argues that whoever the Controller might be, the effects of his individuality are bound to colour the programmes over time. The only logical way to give the Proms the flair that a single imagination can provide — without the otherwise inevitable long-term imbalances affecting both composers and performers — is to appoint a separate planner of the Proms with a limited tenure of four or five years.

Dr Simpson further examines the artistic gains and financial savings to be made from more extensive use of the BBC's own orchestras. Not only would this produce a saving of a staggering 62% on present costs — it would give the planner almost total control over the repertoire. This would enable the Proms to become more adventurous than ever before — a true realisation of Sir Henry Wood's original vision.

'constructive and principled criticism from one of our finest musicians'   Leader, *Daily Telegraph*

'convincing and fierce'   *The Guardian*

'all who are interested in this great annual festival and its future should read this book'   Sir Adrian Boult

vi+66pp; index
£1.95

TOCCATA PRESS
Subscription Scheme

Toccata Press will shortly be launching a subscription scheme for its publications, to include studies of composers, styles, musical institutions and traditions neglected by the 'critical establishment', as well as scholarship offering new insight into familiar masterpieces, often filling surprising gaps in the literature. Toccata Press was founded in the conviction that interest in music of quality is much more widespread than more conventional publishers seem to believe. The subscription scheme will enable musicians and music-lovers to receive on publication every Toccata Press title, usually at a considerable saving.

Several different series have now been planned, principal among these being studies of the music of such composers as Schmidt, Enescu, Medtner, Nielsen, Clementi, Shostakovich, Dussek, Busoni, Bax, Hartmann, Respighi, Sorabji; and there are many more under discussion.

'Musicians on Music', of which *Boult on Music* is No. 1, will assemble writings on music by important composers, performers and writers, often for the first time in English. Among those to be featured are Luigi Dallapiccola, Havergal Brian, Vagn Holmboe and Edmund Rubbra.

'Symphonic Studies' will present detailed but accessible analyses of individual symphonic works, known and unknown, including works by Brahms, Mahler, Nielsen, Magnard, Mozart, Korngold and Beethoven. It will also offer surveys of the symphonies of such composers as Schubert.

Other series will examine the piano literature, investigate the history of style in music, especially early music, and survey the musical achievement of the 20th century country by country. And another will be devoted to operas that have not attracted the attention their stature deserves.

Around eighty titles are already arranged, and these will be sent to subscribers directly upon publication. Many of the titles subscribers will receive are unlikely to appear from any other source, although their musical importance insists on their publication. We hope you will want to be associated with this exciting and pioneering venture; please write for subscription details to:

Toccata Press, 3 Langley Court, London WC2E 9JY.